STAND

COMMIT TO FIGHTING
YOUR SPIRITUAL BATTLE

JOHN GOETSCH

First published in 2014 by Striving Together Publications, a
ministry of Lancaster Baptist Church, Lancaster, CA 93535.
Striving Together Publications is committed to providing
tried, trusted, and proven books that will further equip local
churches to carry out the Great Commission. Your comments
and suggestions are valued.

Striving Together Publications
4020 E. Lancaster Blvd.
Lancaster, CA 93535
800.201.7748

Cover design by Andrew Jones
Layout by Craig Parker
Edited by Monica Bass
Special thanks to our proofreaders

ISBN 978-1-59894-262-0
Printed in the United States of America

Contents

Introduction

Back in Vacation Bible School, spiritual battles seemed so far away—they were always somewhere else, involving someone else. Oh, we learned about spiritual warfare. We studied the pieces of armor. We watched and listened to flannel graph lessons and colored pictures of soldiers. We earned points for memorizing Ephesians 6:10–18:

> *Finally, my brethren, be strong in the Lord, and in the power of his might. Put on the whole armour of God, that ye may be able to stand against the wiles of the devil. For we wrestle not against flesh and blood, but against principalities, against powers, against the rulers of the darkness of this world, against spiritual wickedness in high places. Wherefore take unto you the whole armour of God, that ye may be able to withstand*

in the evil day, and having done all, to stand. Stand
therefore, having your loins girt about with truth, and
having on the breastplate of righteousness; And your
feet shod with the preparation of the gospel of peace;
Above all, taking the shield of faith, wherewith ye shall
be able to quench all the fiery darts of the wicked. And
take the helmet of salvation, and the sword of the Spirit,
which is the word of God: Praying always with all prayer
and supplication in the Spirit, and watching thereunto
with all perseverance and supplication for all saints.
—EPHESIANS 6:10–18

But as children, we felt protected, and we were. We were
protected by our parents, our church, and our leaders. We had
no idea of the lifelong battle that lay before us.

Six decades of life and over forty-five years on the Christian
battlefield later, I find myself in a different position. Many times
over those years, the battle has loomed close and personal,
and the enemy has appeared more real than I ever imagined.
Many of my fellow soldiers have fallen, while others have been
severely wounded.

And while, by the grace of God, I have been able to remain
in the fight, the words of the apostle Paul constantly ring in my
ears: "Wherefore let him that thinketh he standeth take heed lest
he fall" (1 Corinthians 10:12).

A few years ago I spoke at a prophecy conference at First
Baptist Church in Santa Maria, California, where my good friend,
Dr. Jim Schettler was pastoring. I was one of several speakers,

and Dr. Schettler asked me to teach a ninety-minute Tuesday morning overview session on prophecy. It wasn't the topic itself that scared me—it was the fearful task of trying to hold people's attention for an hour and a half early in the morning that was a challenge to my confidence.

After tossing out one idea after another, I decided that preaching in a narrative style, giving the events of prophecy from beginning to end would help keep my listeners awake. Pastor Schettler granted me permission to dress up like the devil and give the narrative from Lucifer's perspective.

I compiled about 450 Bible verses, beginning with the fall of Lucifer from Heaven to his final eternal destruction in Hell. I dressed all in black, wore a goatee, and spiked my hair to give the appearance of horns. The other preachers got a good chuckle at my appearance. Pastor Schettler called from his inner study, "Is Dr. Goetsch here?" The preachers said, "Yes, he just walked in." "What does he look like?" was the next question. Pastor Jeff Redlin replied, "Like a new-evangelical!"

After a few laughs, we knelt around the conference table for a time of prayer. As others began to pray, I silently prayed for God's power and for Him to use the service in the hearts of all who would be present. But, when Pastor Jeff Redlin began to pray, the hair on the back of my neck stood on end. "Dear Lord, please protect Brother Goetsch as he preaches today from the perspective of Satan. We know there will be resistance from the wicked one. Please watch over his wife and children. Please don't let Satan do anything to them...."

By this time I was ready to rip off the goatee and the black turtleneck and forget the whole idea. I suddenly realized I was about to engage in spiritual warfare—and I had been the one to initiate the fight!

God graciously blessed that service with souls saved and Christians encouraged and helped. I haven't preached in that exact style or costume since, but that pre-service prayer meeting was an awakening to me of the reality of spiritual warfare. The truth is, each of us is engaged in a spiritual battle with Satan and his forces every day.

Brother Redlin's prayer also led me to revisit the verses I had memorized as a junior boy in Vacation Bible School. Ephesians 6:10–18 is filled with warning—but it is also about winning. While we, in our own strength, are no match for this spiritual battle, we have a victorious promise in 1 John 4:4: "Ye are of God, little children, and have overcome them: because greater is he that is in you, than he that is in the world."

The purpose of this book is two-fold. First, I pray it warns you, helping you become more aware of the earmarks of the enemy. Second, and just as important, I pray it helps you to win—to come out victorious in the battle.

CHAPTER ONE

The Problem Behind the Problem

A mother and her young son were walking home one evening when a violent thunderstorm developed overhead. The temperature began to drop as ominous clouds rolled in. Rain drops began to fall, and the wind picked up in velocity.

As the two made their way through the city park, the giant oak trees were now whirling in the wind, and small twigs and leaves blew past the hasty travelers. As the little boy looked up and saw the tops of the trees raging like dragons caught by their tails, he said, "Mommy, why don't they cut down these trees so the wind won't blow?"

We smile at the naïve notion of the boy who thinks it is the trees that are causing the wind, but we make the same mistake today. In a world filled with war, violence, crime, hatred, and vice we continue to misunderstand the real problem.

Philosophers, sociologists, politicians, and, yes, many Christians can't seem to discern the difference between the wind and the trees. How many hundreds of atrocities must we endure to understand that the problem is not the trees? How many holocausts? How many Rwandas? How many 9/11s? How many Newtown massacres? How many Boston bombings? The problem is not guns, drugs, mental illness, immigration, or religious cults. These are all *trees*!

Ephesians 6:12 exposes the wind plainly: "For we wrestle not against flesh and blood, but against principalities, against powers, against the rulers of the darkness of this world, against spiritual wickedness in high places."

Christians today who think of the Christian life more as a playground than a battleground even question why God allows all of these tragedies to happen. They see only trees—the visible results of a much deeper problem.

It is time that we discover a biblical worldview concerning evil in this world. In this chapter, we will look at the clearly articulated facts in God's Word regarding the satanic wind that is toppling the trees in our culture today.

G. K. Chesterton once said, "When people begin to say that the material circumstances have alone created the moral circumstances, then they have prevented all possibility of serious change."[1] I would add to Chesterton's observation that

---

1   Gilbert Keith Chesterton, *Tremendous Trifles* (Dodd, Mead and Company, 1920) 92. The illustration of the wind and the trees I have also borrowed from Chesterton, although he used it in a different context than I have.

you and I also prevent all possibility of revival when we cling to cultural views about evil in this world. We dare not accept the sociological, psychological, or political explanations for the evil that now dominates our planet—especially as we have a clear biblical explanation for the "Great War" in which we find ourselves today.

OUR ENEMY

Do you know who Satan is? He doesn't wear a Halloween costume, and he doesn't look like I did when I dressed up in all black with a goatee and spiked hair for horns.

Lucifer was a beautiful, gifted, created angel in Heaven. The prophet Ezekiel describes him for us in this early created state.

*Thou hast been in Eden the garden of God; every precious stone was thy covering, the sardius, topaz, and the diamond, the beryl, the onyx, and the jasper, the sapphire, the emerald, and the carbuncle, and gold: the workmanship of thy tabrets and of thy pipes was prepared in thee in the day that thou wast created. Thou art the anointed cherub that covereth; and I have set thee so: thou wast upon the holy mountain of God; thou hast walked up and down in the midst of the stones of fire. Thou wast perfect in thy ways from the day that thou wast created...—*Ezekiel 28:13–15

God created Lucifer as a powerful angel who had great beauty, gifts, and responsibility. It would seem probable from these verses that he was particularly gifted in music and no doubt led in the worship of God in Heaven. Notice, he was "perfect in all his ways"—that is, until the day when he decided to rebel against God and His preeminence.

The last part of Ezekiel 28:15 says, "...till iniquity was found in thee." There came a day when this gifted angel decided he wanted the preeminence that belonged to God. Isaiah describes the scene for us:

> *How art thou fallen from heaven, O Lucifer, son of the morning! how art thou cut down to the ground, which didst weaken the nations! For thou has said in thine heart, I will ascend into heaven, I will exalt my throne above the stars of God: I will sit also upon the mount of the congregation, in the sides of the north: I will ascend above the heights of the clouds; I will be like the most High.*—ISAIAH 14:12–14

With this rebellion the Great War began!

Challenging God is never a good idea, even if you are a powerful angel. Isaiah aptly describes what happened next: "Yet thou shalt be brought down to hell, to the sides of the pit" (Isaiah 14:15).

God had already decided who would receive all glory in Heaven and in Earth, and it wasn't Lucifer.

Who hath delivered us from the power of darkness, and hath translated us into the kingdom of his dear Son: In whom we have redemption through his blood, even the forgiveness of sins: Who is the image of the invisible God, the firstborn of every creature: For by him were all things created, that are in heaven, and that are in earth, visible and invisible, whether they be thrones, or dominions, or principalities, or powers: all things were created by him, and for him: And he is before all things, and by him all things consist. And he is the head of the body, the church: who is the beginning, the firstborn from the dead; that in all things he might have the preeminence. For it pleased the Father that in him should all fullness dwell;—COLOSSIANS 1:13–19

I'm not sure we understand just how much God hates pride. We speak of certain moral sins today as abominations, and they are described thus in Scripture. But we must be reminded that the "abomination tag" is also placed on the sin of pride: "Every one that is proud in heart is an abomination to the LORD: though hand join in hand, he shall not be unpunished" (Proverbs 16:5). "These six things doth the LORD hate: yea, seven are an abomination unto him: A proud look…" (Proverbs 6:16–17).

There is one name that is exalted above all others—the name of Jesus Christ. Furthermore, God does not and will not give His glory to any other: "I am the LORD: that is my name:

and my glory will I not give to another, neither my praise to graven images" (Isaiah 42:8).

One day, all—including Satan—will acknowledge this Name that is above all names and humble themselves before Him: "Wherefore God also hath highly exalted him, and given him a name which is above every name: That at the name of Jesus every knee should bow, of things in heaven, and things in earth, and things under the earth; And that every tongue should confess that Jesus Christ is Lord, to the glory of God the Father" (Philippians 2:9–11).

Ever since Lucifer was cast out of Heaven for his rebellious pride, he has roamed this universe in absolute defiance against God. He and the fallen angels wage war in every corner of the globe and in each individual heart. To disregard that satanic wind and focus only on the trees is catastrophic!

A CLEVER DECEIVER

Satan may be rebellious, but he isn't stupid. As we study the Great War that began with the fall of Lucifer, it is easy to paint a demonic picture in our minds of this enemy. We have a mental image of a creature that is dreadful, demonic, and destructive. To see an actual being in the likeness of this image would surely cause us to run a hundred miles an hour in the opposite direction! But remember, Satan is brilliant and gifted.

In the book of Proverbs both wisdom and wickedness are personified as a beautiful woman. In the first five verses of chapter 9 we read: "Wisdom hath builded her house, she hath hewn out her seven pillars: She hath killed her beasts; she hath mingled her wine; she hath also furnished her table. She hath sent forth her maidens: she crieth upon the highest places of the city, Whoso is simple, let him turn in hither; as for him that wanteth understanding, she saith to him, Come, eat of my bread, and drink of the wine which I have mingled. Forsake the foolish, and live; and go in the way of understanding."

In chapter 7 we see another kind of woman. Solomon identifies her as the "strange woman" who also with an evil intent entices those who pass near her corner. In chapter 2, his words are pointed as he speaks of her: "To deliver thee from the strange woman, even from the stranger which flattereth with her words; For her house inclineth unto death, and her paths unto the dead. None that go unto her return again, neither take they hold of the paths of life" (Proverbs 2:16, 18–19).

While Satan is certainly wicked, he approaches us in an attractive and desirable way. This is why when the Apostle Paul warned the Corinthian church of false teachers he reminded them that these deceivers were simply following the tactics of their leader. "For such are false apostles, deceitful workers, transforming themselves into the apostles of Christ. And no marvel; for Satan himself is transformed into an angel of light" (2 Corinthians 11:13–14). Satan's greatest tactic is that he often sounds and acts more like God than he does Satan.

If you had been in the garden of Eden with Adam and Eve and had heard God say, "Of every tree of the garden thou mayest freely eat... But of the tree of the knowledge of good and evil, thou shalt not eat of it: for in the day that thou eatest thereof thou shalt surely die" (Genesis 2:16–17), and you heard the serpent say, "…Ye shall not surely die: For God doth know that in the day ye eat thereof, then your eyes shall be opened, and ye shall be as gods, knowing good and evil" (Genesis 3:4–5), who would you have believed?

It seems like a no-brainer that we would listen to the One who created us, rather than some imposter of truth, but Satan is good at what he does. That is why all throughout the Bible, God calls him a *deceiver*. He will continue to employ deception right up to the very end.

> *Let no man deceive you by any means: for that day shall not come, except there come a falling away first, and that man of sin be revealed, the son of perdition; Who opposeth and exalteth himself above all that is called God, or that is worshipped; so that he as God sitteth in the temple of God, shewing himself that he is God. Remember ye not, that, when I was yet with you, I told you these things? And now ye know what withholdeth that he might be revealed in his time. For the mystery of iniquity doth already work: only he who now letteth will let, until he be taken out of the way. And then shall that Wicked be revealed, whom the Lord shall consume with the spirit of his mouth, and shall destroy with the brightness of his coming: Even him, whose coming is after the working of Satan with all power and signs and lying wonders, And with all deceivableness of*

unrighteousness in them that perish; because they received not the love of the truth, that they might be saved.—2 THESSALONIANS 2:3–10

FRAGMENTS OF TRUTH

Have you been wondering what has happened to truth lately? When I was a kid there was a television program called "Truth or Consequences." Indeed, it used to be that to fail to tell the truth brought severe consequences. Today, however, the highest officers in the land lie under oath and get away with it! The prophecy of Isaiah is being fulfilled before our eyes: "In transgressing and lying against the LORD, and departing away from our God, speaking oppression and revolt, conceiving and uttering from the heart words of falsehood. And judgment is turned away backward, and justice standeth afar off: for truth is fallen in the street, and equity cannot enter. Yea, truth faileth; and he that departeth from evil maketh himself a prey: and the LORD saw it, and it displeased him that there was no judgment" (Isaiah 59:13–15).

Truth today has been divided into fact and value. Our culture has accepted the view that absolute truth is only that which is verified by the senses. Empiricism holds to the belief that something is not really true unless you can see, hear, touch, taste, or smell it. If something doesn't meet those standards then it is placed in the camp of value. Thus, God and all theology and morality are determined to be a part of one's values but cannot be verified as fact.

This is why many of our leaders today arrogantly snub their noses at God and religion. They do not believe that there is any "truth" in these matters, but that they are merely a part of some people's values. Today, we can understand Paul's words in Romans 1:25, "Who changed the truth of God into a lie, and worshipped and served the creature more than the Creator, who is blessed for ever. Amen."

Satan is a liar! And you don't have to take my word for it; Jesus Himself said so. In John 8:44 He said, "Ye are of your father the devil, and the lusts of your father ye will do. He was a murderer from the beginning, and abode not in the truth, because there is no truth in him. When he speaketh a lie, he speaketh of his own: for he is a liar, and the father of it."

But remember, even though Satan is a liar, he is very good at what he does. His lie was believable in the garden of Eden, and if we are not careful we can be just as gullible.

THE PROCESS OF DELUSION

Satan doesn't want us to focus on the wind—he works at keeping our attention on the trees. And he has carefully crafted a process which he has used time and again throughout history (with continuing success) to deceive us. We see this process fully played out in Genesis 3.

A Little Discontentment

Think carefully about how God describes the serpent's approach to Eve in the garden: "Now the serpent was more subtil than any beast of the field which the LORD God had made. And he said unto the woman, Yea, hath God said, Ye shall not eat of every tree of the garden?" (Genesis 3:1).

Satan didn't talk to our first parents about all of the wonderful trees that God *did* provide for them in the garden. He rather focused on the one tree that God had not given them. The devil will never focus your mind on the 90 percent of your income that God allows you to use however you choose. He will rather constantly remind you how tough God is being on you to require a tithe. He will never focus your mind on the positive qualities and love of your spouse. He will focus your mind on your spouse's shortcomings.

What has Satan gotten you to focus on lately? Is it something that you believe God has withheld? Perhaps it is a position, a possession, a privilege, a partner, or a prayer unanswered. It is amazing how blinded we can become to all that God has provided and become completely distraught by something He has withheld. We begin to doubt God's love and goodness. We question His authority in our lives. We resist His grace because we are listening to a lie.

God is well aware of this satanic strategy of discontent, and He exhorts us, "Let your conversation be without covetousness: and be content with such things as ye have: for he hath said, I will never leave thee, nor forsake thee" (Hebrews 13:5). The devil makes us believe that we are missing out on something because

God has forbidden some "tree" in our lives. But in reality it is the discontented who lose and the contented who gain.

> *But godliness with contentment is great gain. For we brought nothing into this world, and it is certain we can carry nothing out. And having food and raiment let us be therewith content. But they that will be rich fall into temptation and a snare, and into many foolish and hurtful lusts, which drown men in destruction and perdition. For the love of money is the root of all evil: which while some coveted after, they have erred from the faith, and pierced themselves through with many sorrows.*—1 TIMOTHY 6:6–10

Once Satan creates a little discontentment, the next step is easy for him.

A Lustful Distraction

Once the serpent had convinced Eve that God wasn't good, it wasn't hard for her to notice the forbidden tree. The moment you get your eyes off of the Lord with a little discontentment, Satan will make sure that he has a lustful distraction for you to notice.

> *And when the woman saw that the tree was good for food, and that it was pleasant to the eyes, and a tree to be desired to make one wise, she took of the fruit thereof, and did eat, and gave also unto her husband with her; and he did eat.*—GENESIS 3:6

All Satan has to do is get you to look away from God, and something will be sure to catch your eye!

Notice the word *saw* in the following examples, and notice how these lustful distractions followed a little discontentment:

*And Achan answered Joshua, and said, Indeed I have sinned against the LORD God of Israel, and thus and thus have I done: When I **saw** among the spoils a goodly Babylonish garment, and two hundred shekels of silver, and a wedge of gold of fifty shekels weight, then I coveted them, and took them; and, behold, they are hid in the earth in the midst of my tent, and the silver under it.*
—JOSHUA 7:20–21

*Then went Samson to Gaza and **saw** there an harlot, and went in unto her.*—JUDGES 16:1

*And it came to pass in an eveningtide, that David arose from off his bed, and walked upon the roof of the king's house: and from the roof he **saw** a woman washing herself; and the woman was very beautiful to look upon.*—2 SAMUEL 11:2

Luke 17:32 is a well-known but strange verse: "Remember Lot's wife." What is there to remember about Lot's wife? She is remembered for one thing—she looked back. She didn't *go* back. Satan merely got her to *look* back. No doubt discontented by the command of God to flee the city, she took her eyes off the command and snuck a quick peek back at that which she truly craved.

Where are your eyes today? Are they focused on the Author and Finisher of your faith? Or have you become discontented with God's plan and purpose for your life? You can be sure that when you are discontented, Satan will distract you with something far less valuable and ruin your life. Jesus warned, "No man, having put his hand to the plough, and **looking** back, is fit for the kingdom of God" (Luke 9:62).

A Lost Discernment

Once we start looking in the wrong places we stop looking in the right places.

We naturally lack discernment—so much so that we cannot even accurately evaluate our own hearts. Jeremiah 17:9 warns, "The heart is deceitful above all things, and desperately wicked: who can know it?" Lamentations 3:51 tells us, "Mine eye affecteth mine heart."

So here's the progression so far. We get a little discontent. Then we become distracted by something we see that looks better than what God has provided. Now our hearts are affected and we are well on our way to becoming a casualty, because "…as he thinketh in his heart, so is he…" (Proverbs 23:7).

Sadly, most Christians who are at this point in the process of delusion have dropped out of preaching services and have given up their daily Bible reading. Thus, they have no inputs to spiritual discernment in their lives. When we are there, we even think we are doing fine and "have need of nothing" (Revelation 3:17). In reality, we are about to be destroyed because

Jesus said, "Ye do err, not knowing the scriptures, nor the power of God" (Matthew 22:29).

God's Word is the only remedy for a discontented and distracted heart.

> *For the word of God is quick, and powerful, and sharper than any twoedged sword, piercing even to the dividing asunder of soul and spirit, and of the joints and marrow, and is a discerner of the thoughts and intents of the heart.*—HEBREWS 4:12

> *Whereby are given unto us exceeding great and precious promises: that by these ye might be partakers of the divine nature, having escaped the corruption that is in the world through lust.*—2 PETER 1:4

> *But strong meat belongeth to them that are of full age, even those who by reason of use have their senses exercised to discern both good and evil.*—HEBREWS 5:14

When we sense a little discontentment followed by a lustful distraction, we must get into God's Word for discernment. Failure to do so will result in the final step in Satan's plan.

A Lethal Devouring

First Peter 5:8 warns us, "Be sober, be vigilant; because your adversary the devil, as a roaring lion, walketh about, seeking whom he may devour." The word *devour* here carries the idea of "making to disappear." Satan wants to cause your testimony as a child of God to disappear. He wants to make you ineffective for the cause of Christ and make you spiritually insignificant. Jesus plainly said, "The thief cometh not, but for to steal, and to kill, and to destroy" (John 10:10).

The Lord in a prophetic way warned Peter in Luke 22:31: "And the Lord said, Simon, Simon, behold, Satan hath desired to have you, that he may sift you as wheat." Of course, Peter, being the bold and confident man that he was, scoffed at such a notion. "And he said unto him, Lord, I am ready to go with thee, both into prison, and to death" (Luke 22:33).

But Jesus knew how easy it was for Peter to become discontented, distracted, and lose his discernment; and He rightly predicted his failure in the next verse: "And he said, I tell thee, Peter, the cock shall not crow this day, before that thou shalt thrice deny that thou knowest me."

Sure enough, events unfolded just as the Lord had said: "And Peter said, Man, I know not what thou sayest, And immediately, while he yet spake, the cock crew" (Luke 22:60). Thank God in the next verse, Peter once again came face to face with his Saviour and his discernment returned instantly: "And the Lord turned, and looked upon Peter. And Peter remembered the word of the Lord, how he had said unto him, Before the cock crow, thou shalt deny me thrice. And Peter went out and wept bitterly" (Luke 22:61–62).

Do you feel like Satan has you set up for a fall? Let me encourage you to pick up your Bible immediately and allow God's Word to discern every aspect of your life. Find the house of God and get under the preaching of God's Word. Remember,

"And ye shall know the truth, and the truth shall make you free" (John 8:32).

WHEN THE GREAT WAR ENDS

One day the satanic wind will stop. The devil may be on the prowl today, but he has only a season to accomplish his work. What will ultimately happen to this enemy of God? What is his future?

Scripture tells us that in the end Satan will be cast into a lake of fire: "And the devil that deceived them was cast into the lake of fire and brimstone, where the beast and the false prophet are, and shall be tormented day and night for ever and ever" (Revelation 20:10).

Many people question why a loving God would create a place called Hell. Matthew 25:41 answers that question clearly: "Then shall he say also unto them on the left hand, Depart from me, ye cursed, into everlasting fire, prepared for the devil and his angels." God did not create Hell for people. He created this awful place to punish the rebellious pride of Lucifer and the angels that sinned with him. In fact, God is preparing an entirely different place for people.

> Let not your heart be troubled: ye believe in God, believe also in me. In my Father's house are many mansions: if it were not so, I would have told you. I go to prepare a place for you. And if I go and prepare a place for you,

I will come again, and receive you unto myself; that
where I am, there ye may be also.—JOHN 14:1–3

If you miss Heaven there will be a vacancy there that God
intended you to fill. When people reject Christ as Saviour the
Bible declares in Isaiah 5:14 that Hell must enlarge herself to
accommodate them. Friend, God wants you in Heaven with
Him forever. He created you to have fellowship with Him. Sin
has broken that fellowship, and it can only be restored through
the one and only Saviour, Jesus Christ. In John 14:6 Jesus said,
"I am the way, the truth, and the life: no man cometh unto the
Father, but by me."

He wants you to be saved from your sin and have eternal
life with Him. "For this is good and acceptable in the sight of
God our Saviour; Who will have all men to be saved, and to
come unto the knowledge of the truth" (1 Timothy 2:3–4).

As we have seen, however, Satan is powerful and deceptive.
As a result, many are blinded to his tactics and follow him to a
lake of fire.

And I saw a great white throne, and him that sat on
it, from whose face the earth and the heaven fled way;
and there was found no place for them. And I saw the
dead, small and great, stand before God; and the books
were opened: and another book was opened, which is
the book of life: and the dead were judged out of those
things which were written in the books, according to
their works. And the sea gave up the dead which were in

it; and death and hell delivered up he dead which were in them: and they were judged every man according to their works. And death and hell were cast into the lake of fire. This is the second death. And whosoever was not found written in the book of life was cast into the lake of fire.—REVELATION 20:11–15

Contrary to what a lot of people think and to what many religions teach, there is a Hell and anyone without Christ as his Saviour is going there. "The wicked shall be turned into hell, and all the nations that forget God" (Psalm 9:17). "But the fearful, and unbelieving, and the abominable, and murderers, and whoremongers, and sorcerers, and idolaters, and all liars, shall have their part in the lake which burneth with fire and brimstone: which is the second death" (Revelation 21:8). This is the death that Romans 6:23 speaks of when it says "the wages of sin is death."

Satan will be separated from God once and for all in an eternal abode called Hell. All those who reject Christ as Saviour will suffer that same fate.

Remember, however, no one has to follow the satanic wind. We don't have to be deceived and ultimately suffer a living death forever in a lake of fire called Hell. There is a way of escape. It is not through religion or our own goodness, but rather through a Person—the Lord Jesus Christ.

For the wages of sin is death; but the gift of God is eternal life through Jesus Christ our Lord.—ROMANS 6:23

But God commendeth his love toward us, in that, while we were yet sinners, Christ died for us.—ROMANS 5:8

For whosoever shall call upon the name of the Lord shall be saved.—ROMANS 10:13

And this is the record, that God hath given to us eternal life, and this life is in his Son. He that hath the Son hath life; and he that hath not the Son of God hath not life. These things have I written unto you that believe on the name of the Son of God; that ye may know that ye have eternal life, and that ye may believe on the name of the Son of God.—1 JOHN 5:11–13

But as many as received him, to them gave he power to become the sons of God, even to them that believe on his name.—JOHN 1:12

A LIFE OF FREEDOM

Prior to 1980, the Olmos prison in Argentina was known as the worst of the worst and for the worst. You would not have been allowed to visit because of the dangerous conditions, but if you could have you would have witnessed murders, satanic activity, and violent riots. Today, inmates and guards together can be heard singing and worshipping God.

In the mid-1980s Juan Zuccarelli felt called to prison ministry in this notorious prison. He had preached numbers of crusades in the city of Buenos Aires but had never attempted any type of service in a prison. While daunted by this task, he felt sure that God had called him. He was told, however, that the only way into that prison was as a prison guard. He applied for the position but was told the process would take eight months. Thinking that God surely had closed the door, he was amazed that within a week he was contacted and given the job.

He took the position immediately and organized a preaching service. Three hundred inmates attended, and of those one hundred were gloriously saved. These men, however, were physically, verbally, and sexually assaulted because of their commitment to Christ. Juan was convinced that the Christians needed their own separate cell block where they could meet for Bible study and prayer. He proposed his idea to the prison warden but he was totally against such an idea.

In 1987, Juan discovered an old burnt out cell block that had been completely destroyed years earlier. He told the warden that if he would give him and his Christian followers that cell block, they would fix it to meet the security standards and turn it into the finest cell block in the prison. The warden consented, and a work of God resulted. Twenty-one prisoners started that first cell block and began to have times of prayer, fasting, and Bible study. Eventually, they took over the entire third floor which incidentally up until that time had been called the "Elephant's Floor." It was used to house the most dangerous criminals in Argentina and even had a shrine built in honor of Satan. Family members would bring small animals to the prison for these men to offer as sacrifices to Satan giving him power over the prison. After much prayer and fasting, that entire cell block was inhabited by Christians. In fact, the Christians have twenty-four cell blocks today, and over 1,600 prisoners have been saved at Olmos.

Prisoners at Olmos that have been saved and trained have been sent to other prisons to do the same there. Now, all forty prisons in Argentina have services where the Bible is preached and Jesus Christ is worshipped. Statistics show that 45 percent of all prisoners who are released end up back in prison at some point. In Argentina that number is only 5 percent.

If you don't have a Saviour, today is the day of salvation. Call upon Jesus Christ right now to forgive your sin and give you eternal life.

If you have trusted the Lord as your Saviour, let's find out how we can be victorious in this spiritual warfare. We have an adversary, but the Bible assures us, "…greater is he that is in you, than he that is in the world" (1 John 4:4).

CHAPTER TWO

Battle Zone

Following my freshman year in college I took a job for the summer in northern Wisconsin. I was raised on a dairy farm, but my Dad sold the farm at the end of my senior year in high school. A pastor was planting a church in Gilman, Wisconsin, and came to the college and told of the opportunity to come for the summer and help him with this church plant on Sundays, while working for a farmer in his church throughout the week. I interviewed with the pastor after chapel and took the job "sight unseen" and "boss unseen."

I drove to the little town of Gilman and met Mr. Everett Hettinger, his wife, and small children. The farm was a large operation—way too big for one man to handle especially during the summer months of harvest. We milked nearly one hundred cows twice a day starting at 4:00 AM and in between baled hay, cultivated corn, fixed fences, fed livestock, cleaned barns, painted buildings, and in the middle of the night went fox hunting![1] Mr. Hettinger had been in the Marine Corps and was a physically intimidating man. He was lean and strong and loved the challenge of hard work.

It wasn't long until he discovered that I played football and decided to take it upon himself to get me in shape for the upcoming fall season. He said to me one day: "John, in football you've got to be ready for anything at all times, right? You never know when and from where someone is going to hit you, right? You can't ever let down for a single minute, right?" All of this was true, but I wasn't sure what he was hinting at. He said, "In the Marines, I learned of a little two-letter word. It's the word 'ka.'" (You can look it up. It is an actual word with an Egyptian background and means "your soul.") He said, "When I yell the word 'ka,' you better be ready, because I'm going to attack you!"

As a nineteen year old, I thought I was pretty tough. I kind of chuckled at his proposition and thought to myself, "Yeah right—you and who else?" One early morning as we were making our way across the gravel driveway in front of the house at four in the morning, all of a sudden I heard this demonic scream of "KA!" Within seconds I was lying in the gravel with a 230 pound hulk on top of me screaming and throwing his fists at every part of my body. After pulverizing me, he pushed my face in the gravel, got up and said, "You weren't ready, were you?"

---

1   For those details, read *Homiletics from the Heart* (2003) available from Striving Together Publications.

From that moment on, I realized that Mr. Hettinger was more than serious about this little game of his. He would attack at some of the most unsuspecting times. One evening, I was squatted down inside the stall of a milk cow getting ready to take the milking machine off of her when he sneaked up from behind, yelled "KA!" and started beating me with a milking stool! The cow spooked and started kicking and bucking. The milking machine went flying as two grown men were in a wrestling match underneath a very nervous and irritated animal. It was difficult the next morning to figure out which bruises were from Betsy and which ones were from her owner.

We had some pretty intense battles that summer, and one day, Mr. Hettinger invited me outside where he had drawn a large circle in the gravel driveway in front of the house. He had each of his kids along with his wife standing around that circle like security at the White House. He said, "Today, we're going to see who's tougher—you or me. When my wife yells 'KA!' everything goes. No holds barred. The last one inside this circle is the winner. Without a chance to warm up or check with my agent, his wife yelled that infamous word and the battle was on!

I'm not sure how long we were in that circle but every fighting tactic ever thought of by humanity was in full use that day. Punching, clawing, scratching, biting, kicking, and pushing as two grown men battled for victory. I didn't know much about this kind of street fighting, but football had taught me about getting leverage. The low man always wins and because I was smaller and shorter than Mr. Hettinger, I was able to use that one small advantage against him. He didn't lose happily and

I probably lost more than I won that day. (He refused to pay me my wages for the summer.) Years later we met again, shook hands, and had a lot of good laughs over our battles.

Whether or not that experience helped me in football I'm not sure, but I know it taught me something about spiritual warfare. We must be battle ready. Our enemy waits for that moment when we are not sober or vigilant.

The moment we get saved we enter into spiritual warfare. This is not simply Satan against Christianity as a whole, but Satan against each individual child of God. In describing this combat in Ephesians 6, the Apostle Paul says in verse 12, "For we wrestle...." Wrestling is a close one-on-one contact sport.

Do you understand that you are in an intense war? Notice the emphasis of warfare in the following verses.

> *But I see another law in my members, **warring** against the law of my mind, and bringing me into captivity to the law of sin which is in my members.*—ROMANS 7:23

> *For the weapons of our **warfare** are not carnal, but mighty through God to the pulling down of strongholds;*—2 CORINTHIANS 10:4

> *This charge I commit unto thee, son Timothy, according to the prophecies which went before on thee, that thou by them mightest **war** a good **warfare**.*—1 TIMOTHY 1:18

> *No man that **warreth** entangleth himself with the affairs of this life; that he may please him who hath chosen him to be a soldier.*—2 TIMOTHY 2:4

*Fight the good **fight** of faith…*—1 TIMOTHY 6:12

*I have **fought** a good **fight**…*—2 TIMOTHY 4:7

The battlefield is all around us. There are no rules, no time limit, no referee—it's a matter of life or death.

As in any battle, it is vital that we understand what we are up against—the arena of the battlefield. In this chapter, we'll identify where the battle lies and the fierceness of the opposition we face.

A SHROUDED BATTLEFIELD

As a hurricane, tornado, or violent thunderstorm moves through an area, no one sees the wind—only the damage left behind. So it is in spiritual warfare. We do not see the forces in the battlefield surrounding us; we only see the effects of those forces. This is true concerning *both* sides in the war.

As Jesus explained the new birth to Nicodemus, He used the wind as an illustration of the Holy Spirit: "The wind bloweth where it listeth, and thou hearest the sound thereof, but canst not tell whence it cometh, and whither it goeth" (John 3:8).

In coming chapters, we'll study more fully the work of the Holy Spirit and the weapons He has given us for this war. But for now, notice that just because we cannot see Him at work does not mean He is absent. We see the effects of His work within our own lives.

Similarly, we cannot see Satan—yet, he too is at work. Ephesians 6:12 tells us, "For we wrestle not against flesh and blood, but against principalities, against powers, against the rulers of the darkness of this world, against spiritual wickedness in high places."

This obscurity of our enemy provides a challenge for us in that we must always be vigilant. When Mr. Hettinger was on the back forty cutting alfalfa and I was up at the barn feeding cattle, I didn't have to worry about an attack. It was only when I was in his physical presence that I had to be vigilant. But this is not the case with our enemy. We can't see him, but we must be on our guard against him.

DON'T MISTAKE THE TARGET

Satan uses his invisibility to his advantage. One of his greatest tactics is to get us to focus on the wrong target. Because we can't see him, but we can see the people who stand in our way, Satan uses those people as decoys—focusing our attention on *them* as the enemy rather than on himself.

I'm sure this was the case in the early church at Jerusalem that we read about in the book of Acts: "And Saul, yet breathing out threatenings and slaughter against the disciples of the Lord, went unto the high priest, And desired of him letters to Damascus to the synagogues, that if he found any of this way, whether they were men or women, he might bring them bound unto Jerusalem" (Acts 9:1–2).

Saul of Tarsus was a zealous Pharisee who took it upon himself to wipe out Christianity in the first century. Not only did he harass the believers, he even ordered some to be put to death. In Acts 8, following the martyrdom of Stephen, we read: "And Saul was consenting unto his death. And at that time there was a great persecution against the church which was at Jerusalem; and they were all scattered broad throughout the regions of Judaea and Samaria, except the apostles" (Acts 8:1). In Paul's testimony to King Agrippa later, Paul confesses, "I verily thought with myself, that I ought to do many things contrary to the name of Jesus of Nazareth. Which thing I also did in Jerusalem: and many of the saints did I shut up in prison, having received authority from the chief priests; and when they were put to death, I gave my voice against them. And I punished them oft in every synagogue, and compelled them to blaspheme; and being exceedingly mad against them, I persecuted them even unto strange cities" (Acts 26:9–11).

I wonder if anyone in the early church was praying that God would kill Saul or at the least remove him from his place of authority? To these persecuted Christians, the battlefield looked clearly marked: They were on one side doing the work of God, and Saul, their enemy, was on the other side destroying the work of God.

But by Acts 17, this "enemy" had been saved and "had turned the world upside down" for Christ!

When we see a person as our enemy, we totally mistake the target in spiritual warfare. We spend our time hacking away at trees, rather than addressing the wind.

I remind you, Ephesians 6:12 plainly says, "For we wrestle not against flesh and blood...." The enemy is not your spouse or your parent; or your boss or a Supreme Court justice or even the President of the United States! These are only trees. Even as they may now be trees bending to the forces of Satan, they, like Saul of Tarsus, may later become trees bending to the will of God. In fact, God may use those very people to lead the next great revival.

Nebuchadnezzar was perhaps the most powerful king who ever sat on a throne anywhere in this world. The prophet Daniel reviews the mighty power held by this king: "...the most high God gave Nebuchadnezzar thy father a kingdom, and majesty, and glory, and honour: And for the majesty that he gave him, all people, nations, and languages, trembled and feared before him: whom he would he slew; and whom he would he kept alive; and whom he would he set up; and whom he would he put down" (Daniel 5:18–19).

This mighty king threw three men in a fire because they wouldn't bow down to his statue. This was a dictatorship with phony laws trumped up to wipe out God's people. It was arrogant and self-serving government at its best!

But notice the words of this same king in Daniel 3:28–29: "Then Nebuchadnezzar spake, and said, Blessed be the God of Shadrach, Meshach, and Abednego, who hath sent his angel, and delivered his servants that trusted in him, and have changed the king's word, and yielded their bodies, that they might not serve nor worship any god, except their own God. Therefore I make a decree, That every people, nation, and language, which speak any thing amiss against the God of Shadrach, Meshach, and Abednego, shall be cut in pieces, and their houses shall be made a dunghill: because there is no other God that can deliver after this sort."

The satanic wind is the enemy—the hearts of the "trees" are in the hand of the Lord. We must not mistake our enemy.

KNOW YOUR WEAPONS

Because we too often mistake our enemy, we select faulty weapons with which to win the battle. Specifically, we trust ourselves and our resources. We look to our weapons, our strategy, or our experience, to win a war humanly against a non-human opponent.

Paul reminds us, "For the weapons of our warfare are not carnal, but mighty through God to the pulling down of strong holds" (2 Corinthians 10:4). The word *carnal* here refers to our flesh or our own human abilities. Those weapons are insufficient in spiritual warfare.

Not only are we in trouble against Satan when we use our fleshly weapons, but we anger God as well.

> *Thus saith the LORD; Cursed be the man that trusteth in man, and maketh flesh his arm, and whose heart departeth from the LORD.*—JEREMIAH 17:5

> *Woe to them that go down to Egypt for help; and stay on horses, and trust in chariots, because they are many;*

and in horsemen, because they are very strong; but they
look not unto the Holy One of Israel, neither seek the
LORD!—ISAIAH 31:1

This battle is not fair. The sides are not equal. You are up against Goliath. So what are you trusting? Your slingshot? The fact that you killed a bear once? Or a lion? The little shepherd boy, David, had indeed killed a bear and a lion with his bare hands and he was pretty good with that slingshot, but as he approached the battle, his trust was in Someone much stronger than all of those human resources: "And all this assembly shall know that the LORD saveth not with sword and spear: for the battle is the LORD's, and he will give you into our hands" (1 Samuel 17:47).

We have been given one weapon for this battle—and most of us have no idea where it is when we need it.

Your enemy is powerful. You can't out-muscle him. You can't out-smart him. You can't out-run him or out-shout him. But you can out-truth him! This is why Ephesians 6:17 instructs, "And take...the sword of the Spirit, which is the word of God."

If you know one Bible verse, you have more truth than your enemy. "He was a murderer from the beginning, and abode not in the truth, because there is no truth in him" (John 8:44).

You are in a spiritual war and are surrounded by a powerful and gifted enemy. Do you have your weapon ready? Satan is not going to let you call your pastor before he attacks. He's not going to let you get out your concordance in the middle of the war. You must have Scripture memorized and ready. The psalmist said, "Thy word have I hid in mine heart, that I might not sin against thee" (Psalm 119:11).

Back in the 1980s I was preaching for the first time in Honolulu, Hawaii. The Ohana Baptist Church had a large number of military men and women from various branches of the service in their congregation. One night after the service, several men invited me to play racquetball with them up at Fort Smith. I grabbed a change of clothes and went with them on to the base. For the next two hours, we enjoyed some intense competition.

Around midnight, a few of the guys needed to either go to work or get rest for the next day, and so we walked out into the cool night air to go our separate ways. One of the gentlemen, a high ranking officer in the Marine Corps, said, "Brother Goetsch, let's go for a jog!"

"Are you joking?" I said. "It's midnight!"

"Come on, don't be a wimp," he yelled as he started off running.

I took the challenge, and we jogged all through that base and chatted about a number of things as we did. I asked him what he did in the Marine Corps. He informed me that he was in charge of all of the weapons in the South Pacific. On his computer in his office at Fort Smith, he could locate every weapon that the US military had in the entire region and could activate any of them at a moment's notice!

Somehow, I felt very safe that night as we jogged.

Do you know where *your* weapon is? When Jesus was tempted by Satan in the wilderness (Matthew 4:1–11), He had

His weapon ready. Every time the devil came with a temptation, Jesus responded with an Old Testament verse.

Indeed, God's Word *is* truth. This powerful weapon is the only weapon we have against our deadly foe.

> *The prophet that hath a dream, let him tell a dream; and he that hath my word, let him speak my word faithfully. What is the chaff to the wheat? saith the LORD. Is not my word like as a fire? saith the LORD; and like a hammer that breaketh the rock in pieces?*—JEREMIAH 23:28–29

Satan has no counter move to God's Word.

> *For we can do nothing against the truth, but for the truth.*—2 CORINTHIANS 13:8

> *…thy word is truth.*—JOHN 17:17

INVISIBLE…BUT ORGANIZED

We may not be able to see our enemies, but believe me, they are not invisible to each other. Remember, we are not battling some snarly little guy with a goatee, pitchfork, and horns. We're battling a well-entrenched, thoroughly-organized force. Let's take a look at the layers of organization, spelled out for us in Ephesians 6:12: "For we wrestle not against flesh and blood, but against principalities, against powers, against the rulers of the darkness of this world, against spiritual wickedness in high places."

God informs us of four classifications within the ranks of our enemy. He first mentions *principalities*. The Greek word here is *archas* and means "head ones" or "powerful ones."

He then speaks of *powers*. Here the word is *exousia*. These are characterized by inward ability and endowment.

Then we see the phrase *rulers of darkness*. Two Greek words are used here: *Cosmos* meaning "world," and *kratas* meaning "power." These "cosmo kratoras" or "world powers" are the force behind the holocausts, the 9/11s, the Boston bombings, etc. They are the rulers of the darkness of this world.

Finally, He calls our attention to *spiritual wickedness in high places*. These are the *pneumatika* or spiritual beings of wickedness in the heavens.

The whole earth is covered with these unseen and invisible enemies of darkness. How did this happen? Certainly God did not create this. How did we get to the place where we are surrounded by wicked beings ready to do spiritual warfare against us?

Let's take a moment for a brief Bible study on angels because it will give us the background we need to understand this invisible force of evil.

Angels are identified several different ways in Scripture. Some are called *seraphim*. The Hebrew word means "burning ones." They stand continuously in God's presence and worship Him. We notice them in Isaiah 6:1–3: "In the year that king Uzziah died I saw also the Lord sitting upon a throne, high and lifted up, and his train filled the temple. Above it stood the seraphims: each one had six wings; with twain he covered his face, and with twain he covered his feet, and with twain he did fly. And one cried unto another, and said, Holy, holy, holy, is the LORD of hosts: the whole earth is full of his glory."

Very early in the Bible record we are introduced to angels called *cherubim*. They were placed at the eastern gate of the garden of Eden and are called "living ones." "So he drove out the man; and he placed at the east of the garden of Eden Cherubims, and a flaming sword which turned every way, to keep the way of the tree of life" (Genesis 3:24). Cherubim are symbols of God's love, grace, mercy, and forgiveness.

Then we have angels who are identified individually by name. Michael is called the archangel. One day we will hear his voice! "For the Lord himself shall descend from heaven with a shout, with the voice of the archangel, and with the trump of God: and the dead in Christ shall rise first" (1 Thessalonians 4:16). Michael is mentioned five times in the Bible—three times in Daniel, and once each in Jude and Revelation. Michael stands as the guardian angel for God's people.

The angel Gabriel is also mentioned by name and is the messenger of God. We recall that it was this angel who appeared to Zacharias and announced the birth of John the Baptist: "And there appeared unto him an angel of the Lord standing on the right side of the altar of incense. And when Zacharias saw him, he was troubled, and fear fell upon him. But the angel said unto him, Fear not, Zacharias: for thy prayer is heard; and thy wife Elisabeth shall bear thee a son, and thou shalt call his name John" (Luke 1:11–13). Gabriel is mentioned four times in Scripture and always is identified with the redemptive work of Jesus Christ.

After mentioning these specific angels, the Bible then speaks of an uncountable number of other angels. They were created by God from the foundation of the world and rejoiced at His creation of the world. They will one day welcome us into Heaven and will spend eternity with us. Hebrews 12:22 says, "But ye are come unto mount Sion, and unto the city of the living God, the heavenly Jerusalem, and to an innumerable company of angels."

We see the vast number of these angels emphasized in Revelation 5:11: "And I beheld, and I heard the voice of many angels round about the throne and the beasts and the elders: and the number of them was ten thousand times ten thousand, and thousands and thousands." The word used here for *thousands* is a word that we get our English word *myriad* from—literally an uncountable number. Ten myriads times ten myriads and myriads and myriads!

God has given these angels a great deal of power. In 2 Chronicles 32:1 we read where "Sennacherib, king of Assyria, came, and entered into Judah, and encamped against the fenced cities, and thought to win them for himself." In verse 20 of the same chapter we read, "And for this cause Hezekiah the king, and the prophet Isaiah the son of Amoz, prayed and cried to heaven." The result of that prayer meeting was amazing! "And the LORD sent an angel, which cut off all the mighty men of valour, and the leaders and captains in the camp of the king of Assyria..." (2 Chronicles 32:21). Isaiah recalling that story in Isaiah 37:36 gives us the number that the angel smote that night—185,000! One angel wiped out 185,000 men in answer to prayer!

On the night of Jesus' betrayal, we find Peter boldly trying to protect Jesus from those who were coming to arrest Him. You might recall that Peter pulls out his sword and takes off the ear of Malchus—one of the high priest's servants. Jesus' response is classic: "Then said Jesus unto him, Put up again thy sword into his place: for all they that take the sword shall perish with the sword. Thinkest thou that I cannot now pray to my Father, and he shall presently give me more than twelve legions of angels?" (Matthew 26:52–53).

Think about what Jesus just said. One legion in the Roman army consisted of 6,000 soldiers, so twelve legions would translate to 72,000 soldiers. Jesus at that moment had access to 72,000 angels. It only took one angel to kill 185,000 in Hezekiah's day. Jesus had 72,000 angels at His beck and call…and Simon Peter was worried about Malchus!

These angels live amongst us; they work with us; they guide us, guard us, and keep us. They are the ministering spirits of Heaven. But as we noted in Chapter 1, there was a particular angel who rebelled against God. He is identified as Lucifer, the deceiver, and undoubtedly the most powerful angel of all. Even Michael the archangel wanted nothing to do with Lucifer as they argued about the body of Moses: "Yet Michael the archangel, when contending with the devil he disputed about the body of Moses, durst not bring against him a railing accusation, but said, The Lord rebuke thee" (Jude 9). He is called "an angel of light" in 2 Corinthians 11:14 and the "god of this world" in 2 Corinthians 4:4. He is brilliant, shrewd, gifted, strategic, and almost invincible. And it is he, Satan, who leads the attack against us in this spiritual warfare.

But Satan does not operate alone. The book of Revelation gives us some insight into the fall of Lucifer from Heaven that we studied in Isaiah 14 and Ezekiel 28: "And there appeared another wonder in heaven; and behold a great red dragon, having seven heads and ten horns, and seven crowns upon his heads. And his tail drew a third part of the stars of heaven, and did cast them to the earth…" (Revelation 12:3–4).

When Lucifer rebelled against God, he influenced one third of the angels to resist with him and thus they too were cast out of Heaven with the devil.

> *And there was war in heaven: Michael and his angels fought against the dragon; and the dragon fought and his angels, And prevailed not; neither was their place found any more in heaven. And the great dragon was cast out, that old serpent, called the Devil, and Satan, which deceiveth the whole world: he was cast out into the earth, and his angels were cast out with him.*
> —REVELATION 12:7–9

These angels are here now—in our battle zone.

ACTIVE DUTY

Satan and these fallen angels are never in "reserve ranks." They are both active and busy in a whole host of threats and attacks.

In Job 1:7, God and Satan are having a conversation: "And the LORD said unto Satan, Whence comest thou? Then Satan answered the LORD, and said, From going to and fro in the earth, and walking up and down in it." No, Satan doesn't sit on his hands. He's busy in our arena of battle.

I shudder when I read the words in Zechariah 3:1: "And he shewed me Joshua the high priest standing...and Satan standing at his right hand ready to resist him." When a servant of God stands to preach, no doubt Satan or one of his angels stands at his right hand ready to resist all that is declared. They resist our witness, our testimony, our ministry.

The Apostle Paul identified his "thorn in the flesh" as a "messenger of Satan" in 2 Corinthians 12:7. I have no doubt that one of these messengers is assigned to our children to try to lead them in rebellion against their parents. Perhaps they are assigned to marriages to cause heartache and ruin. They sit in our church services ready to resist the Spirit of God and His work in the hearts of the lost as well as the saved.

This army of fallen angels has one goal—to destroy! They have an insatiable appetite for destruction. They follow their leader who is "a murderer from the beginning" (John 8:44) and want nothing less than to "devour" us, as 1 Peter 5:8 reminds us. They are experts at what they do.

Death is universal, as is pain, misery, and heartache. Disease and suffering know no boundaries. Humanity under Satan's direction walks a dark and tormenting path that ends for most in the darkness of the grave and an everlasting lake of fire.

The goal of Satan is simple—death forever in Hell with him. He may be obscure, but he is organized in all that he does to accomplish his purpose.

OBSTINATE AT EVERY TURN

Satan won a huge victory in the Garden of Eden. He deceived our first parents, and they fell from God's presence and fellowship because of their sin. The Bible teaches that when they did, every person who would come after them would be born contaminated with the sin nature: "Wherefore, as by one man sin entered into the world, and death by sin; and so death passed upon all men, for that all have sinned" (Romans 5:12). The Bible comes to a conclusion about the condition of the human race: "But the scripture hath concluded all under sin…" (Galatians 3:22).

God, however, designed a wonderful plan of redemption. My favorite verse in the Bible is 2 Samuel 14:14: "For we must needs die, and are as water spilt on the ground, which cannot be gathered up again; neither doth God respect any person: yet doth he devise means, that his banished be not expelled from him." You and I are like water spilt on the ground. You have no doubt heard the expression, "There's no sense crying over spilled milk!" That phrase comes from the Bible, and it describes our lives. We only get one chance at life—there is no such thing as reincarnation or a second chance ("…it is appointed unto men once to die…" Hebrews 9:27). And, God is no respecter of persons when it comes to death. Young people die as frequently as the elderly. Healthy people die as well as those who are ill. But God in His great love for the human race devised a means by which when man dies he does not have to be separated from God for all of eternity but can be brought back into fellowship with God.

What was this means that God devised? "For God so loved the world, that he gave his only begotten Son, that whosoever believeth in him should not perish, but have everlasting life" (John 3:16). God's only Son became the means whereby you and I could be redeemed! "But God commendeth his love toward us, in that, while we were yet sinners, Christ died for us" (Romans 5:8).

This wonderful gift that God has provided is not automatically passed out to all in the human race, but must be received personally by each individual. What a wonderful relationship is established however, when a person receives that gift! John 1:12 says, "But as many as received him, to them gave he power to become the sons of God, even to them that believe on his name."

As God carried out this plan of redemption, it only intensified the battle between God and Satan. The devil opposed and warred against every step in the redemptive plan.

Several years ago, a church where I was preaching made arrangements for me to attend a performance at Sight and Sound in Lancaster, Pennsylvania. They presented the life of Joseph, and I enjoyed it immensely. As a speech and drama major in college, I thrilled not only at the story, but at the technical aspects of the performance. The gospel was clearly presented at the end, and I was determined to return and see another play presented at my first opportunity.

Some months later, my wife was with me on the East Coast during the Christmas season, and we made arrangements to attend the *Christmas Story* at Sight and Sound. There was one particular scene that I will never forget. It actually became the catalyst to the material in this book. It was the manger scene in Bethlehem the night Jesus was born.

In the drama, as Mary went into labor in the stable, Joseph became concerned and called for the innkeeper's wife to come and help with the delivery of the baby. As Mary sobbed and the innkeeper's wife tried to help, it was obvious that something was wrong.

Suddenly from high above the set floor, a dark and ominous angel came flying in and took a position above that stable with his sword drawn. As he hovered over the stable (suspended by wires that could barely be seen), he grinned with satisfaction as he attempted to abort God's redemptive plan.

Mary was now sobbing, Joseph was frantic, and the innkeeper's wife was calling for her husband to please help. Then in a flash from the ceiling at stage right came a beautiful and powerful angel who began to do battle with the dark angel. Their swords clashed above that stable for a few moments, and then Michael the archangel thrust a blow to the heart of the dark angel who went tumbling off into the sky in the opposite direction. As Michael stood in triumph over the stable, the baby

Jesus was delivered to the joy of those in the scene and in reality to the joy of all mankind.

When the scene closed, I must admit that my first thought was, "Where is that in the Bible?" But while that description of warfare is not written with words in the Scriptures, we see the opposition is portrayed clearly at every stage in God's plan of salvation.

How did Satan oppose God's plan of redemption?

He Opposed His Arrival

Satan and his fallen angels began to strategize the moment they heard the words, "And she shall bring forth a son, and thou shalt call his name JESUS: for he shall save his people from their sins" (Matthew 1:21).

We see Satan developing his plan as the wise men stood before Herod: "Then Herod, when he had privily called the wise men, enquired of them diligently what time the star appeared. And he sent them to Bethlehem, and said, Go and search diligently for the young child: and when ye have found him, bring me word again, that I may come and worship him also" (Matthew 2:7–8). But God knew the heart of Herod and the satanic plot that was developing, and He thwarted it: "And being warned of God in a dream that they should not return to Herod, they departed into their own country another way" (Matthew 2:12).

Reeling from this blow, Satan now moves Herod's heart to commit one of the most hideous crimes in the history of mankind: "Then Herod, when he saw that he was mocked of the wise men, was exceeding wroth, and sent forth, and slew all the children that were in Bethlehem, and in all the coasts thereof, from two years old and under, according to the time which he had diligently enquired of the wise men" (Matthew 2:16).

Satan did everything in his power to keep the Saviour from entering this world because he knew why Jesus had come: "For the Son of man is come to seek and to save that which was lost" (Luke 19:10). Satan failed but he didn't give up.

He Opposed His Authority

As Jesus begins His earthly ministry we find the imps of Satan opposing Him at every turn. They knew who the Son of God was which is evident by their conversations with Him.

> And there was in their synagogue a man with an
> unclean spirit; and he cried out, Saying, Let us alone;
> what have we to do with thee, thou Jesus of Nazareth?
> art thou come to destroy us? I know thee who thou art,
> the Holy One of God.—MARK 1:23–24

The legion of devils living in the body of the maniac in Mark 5 also knew who Jesus was and the authority He possessed.

> But when he saw Jesus afar off, he ran and worshipped
> him, And cried with a loud voice, and said, What have
> I to do with thee, Jesus, thou Son of the most high God?
> I adjure thee by God, that thou torment me not. For
> he said unto him, Come out of the man, thou unclean

spirit. And he asked him, What is thy name? And he
answered, saying, my name is Legion: for we are many.
—MARK 5:6–9

This is why James tells us in James 2:19, "...the devils also believe, and tremble." They knew the authority that Jesus Christ possessed and opposed Him every chance they had. "And devils also came out of many, crying out, and saying, Thou art Christ the Son of God. And he rebuking them suffered them not to speak: for they knew that he was Christ" (Luke 4:41).

He Opposed His Atonement

Every step that Christ took toward the cross involved spiritual warfare. Satan had planted an enemy within the very circle of the disciples. "Now before the feast of the Passover, when Jesus knew that his hour was come that he should depart out of this world unto the Father, having loved his own which were in the world, he loved them unto the end. And supper being ended, the devil having now put into the heart of Judas Iscariot, Simon's son, to betray him" (John 13:1–2).

It was Satan who brought that sleep of carelessness over the disciples in the Garden of Gethsemane as Jesus was sweating "as it were great drops of blood." It was Satan who motivated that betrayal kiss on the face of the Son of God by the imposter disciple. You could hear Satan's voice in the howling crowd as they cried, "Crucify him; Away with him." It was Satan's hands that guided those of the Roman soldiers as they scourged Him and plucked His beard. It was Satan's spittle that ran down Christ's face as the crowd spit on and mocked Him. The venomous words hurled His way were from Satan's vocabulary. Satan laughed as the nails pierced Christ's hands and feet. He squealed with glee when Jesus gave up the ghost. He watched with careful eye as the tomb was sealed and the Roman guards took their post.

Satan thought he had won. But on that third day, Christ arose. Still, Satan made one last attempt to stop Him.

He Opposed His Ascension

Foiled in the Garden of Eden, Satan thought he had Christ trapped in the wilderness as he came to tempt Him. He thought he had corralled His power as the arrest was made in the garden of Gethsemane. Satan had the government on his side in Pilate's Judgment Hall. He had the crowd in a frenzy as they howled at Golgotha. He was sure of victory as the tomb was sealed. But alas, he failed as Jesus conquered death and the grave. Now as Jesus ascends back to His Father, the wicked one seeks to block His return to glory.

But Jesus Christ went right through the organized ranks! He overpowered the principalities, and powers, and the rulers of darkness, and even the spiritual wickedness in the surrounding heavens. Listen to the powerful and victorious words in Ephesians 1:19–21: "And what is the exceeding greatness of his power to us-ward who believe, according to the working of his mighty power. Which he wrought in Christ, when he raised him from the dead, and set him at his own right hand in the heavenly places, Far above all principality, and power, and might, and dominion, and every name that is named, not only in this world, but also in that which is to come."

Failing miserably in his attempt to stop this plan of redemption, Satan now turns his attention to us.

YOUR SOUL—A MUTUAL PRIZE

We are not a part of God's family simply because we are a part of the human race. In fact, the Bible says we are separated from God in our natural condition.

> *Wherein in time past ye walked according to the course of this world, according to the prince of the power of the air, the spirit that now worketh in the children of disobedience. Among whom also we all had our conversation in times past in the lusts of our flesh, fulfilling the desires of the flesh and of the mind; and were by nature the children of wrath, even as others.*
> —Ephesians 2:2–3

We cannot enter this family of God through our bloodline, our good deeds, or by sheer will power: "Which were born, not of blood, nor of the will of the flesh, nor of the will of man, but of God" (John 1:13).

The only way into God's family is by an adoption process made possible by God's Son. Galatians 4:3–5 speaks of this: "Even so we, when we were children, were in bondage under the elements of the world: But when the fullness of time was come, God sent forth his Son, made of a woman, made under the law, To redeem them that were under the law, that we might receive the adoption of sons."

But Satan opposes this process just as he opposed Christ. You see, the prize in this spiritual warfare is your soul! Satan wants it! God wants it! John 10:10 clearly identifies the target for both Satan and God: "The thief cometh not, but for to steal, and to kill, and to destroy: I am come that they might have life, and that they might have it more abundantly."

VICTORY IN THE ARENA

Satan wants to destroy us—God wants to give us victory. So, how do we get on the winning side? How do we win this spiritual battle?

Notice the instruction in Revelation 12:10–11: "And I heard a loud voice saying in heaven, Now is come salvation, and strength, and the kingdom of our God, and the power of his Christ: for the accuser of our brethren is cast down, which accused them before our God day and night. And they overcame him by the blood of the Lamb, and by the word of their testimony; and they loved not their lives unto the death."

We discover here the first three steps to victory in spiritual warfare: first, they overcame him by the blood of the Lamb. Have you been washed in the blood of the Lamb? Victory starts with salvation. We must do something about our sin.

The problem is that there is nothing we can do to delete sin from our lives. There is only one solution.

But now in Christ Jesus ye who sometimes were far off are made nigh by the blood of Christ.—EPHESIANS 2:13

And almost all things are by the law purged with blood; and without shedding of blood is no remission.—HEBREWS 9:22

...the blood of Jesus Christ his Son cleanseth us from all sin.—1 JOHN 1:7

Jesus Christ shed His blood to provide an atonement for our sin. Have you asked Him to be your Saviour; to forgive your sins; and give you eternal life? There is no victory without this vital first step of salvation.

Second, they overcame him with the word of their testimony. Once we are saved by faith, God commands us to live by faith. Philippians 1:27 exhorts, "Let your conversation be as it becometh the gospel of Christ." The way that we live (our conversation) ought to resemble the Person of the Lord Jesus Christ. When we allow Christ to live through us in our daily walk, we will have victory over the attacks of Satan. "For this is the love of God, that we keep his commandments; and his commandments are not grievous. For whatsoever is born of God overcometh the world: and this is the victory that overcometh the world, even our faith" (1 John 5:3–4). As we surrender each area of our lives to Christ and live as He commands us—victory is assured. "Submit yourselves therefore to God. Resist the devil, and he will flee from you" (James 4:7).

Third, Revelation 12 tells us that they loved not their lives to the death. We cannot win this war if we are only in the battle halfway. This battle demands our full attention. It will take a commitment like that of the Apostle Paul when he said, "But none of these things move me, neither count I my life dear unto myself, so that I might finish my course with joy, and the ministry, which I have received of the Lord Jesus, to testify the gospel of the grace of God" (Acts 20:24). If you are willing to die for the Lord, you will have no trouble living for Him!

The first-century Christian, Polycarp, stood before the proconsul (a governor over a Roman state) for his faith in Christ. "Take the oath and I will let you go," the proconsul urged. "Revile Christ."

Polycarp responded, "For eighty and six years have I been His servant, and He has done me no wrong, and how can I blaspheme my King who saved me?"

At this statement the crowd cried out in uncontrollable wrath: "This is the teacher of Asia, the father of the Christians, the destroyer of our gods, who teaches many neither to offer sacrifice nor to worship."

The proconsul was commanded to let loose a lion on Polycarp, but he said he could not legally do so because he had already closed the sports.

The demand was then made for this man of God to be burnt alive. Once the command was given, the howling and vicious crowd flew into action. They gathered wood and faggots from the woodshops, and the fire was made ready. Polycarp loosened his clothes and girdle and tried to take off his shoes. He was now fastened to the instruments which had been prepared for the fire, but when they began to nail him to the wood, he said, "Leave me thus, for He who gives me power to endure the fire, will grant me to remain in the flames unmoved even without the security you will give by the nails."

Now this battle-tested believer lifted his voice in prayer: "I bless Thee, that Thou hast granted me this day and hour, that I may share, among the number of the martyrs, in the cup of Christ. May I today, be received among them before Thee, as a rich and acceptable sacrifice, as Thou, the God who lies not and is truth, hast prepared beforehand, and shown forth, and fulfilled. For this reason I also praise Thee for all things, I bless Thee, I glorify Thee through the everlasting and heavenly High Priest, Jesus Christ, through whom be glory to Thee, both now and for the ages that are to come, Amen."

When he finished his prayer, the men in charge of the fire lit it, and a great flame blazed up, but to the onlookers an amazing thing took place. The fire made the likeness about Polycarp like a room; like the sail of a vessel filled with wind. It surrounded the body of the martyr like a wall around him, but he himself was unharmed. Soon, the men who called for his death, seeing that his body could not be consumed by the fire, commanded an executioner to go and stab him with a dagger. As this was done, so much blood came out of the wound that it quenched the fire. Polycarp gave his life for Christ, and the crowd marveled that there was such a difference in the death of the believers and the nonbelievers.

Today, none of us are being led to an arena filled with blood-thirsty enemies to be burned alive. But we are required each day to live before a crowd of people around us that is often fueled with its animosity by the same source. Does anyone marvel that there is such a difference between the way believers live as opposed to the way unbelievers live? In 2 Corinthians 3:2–3, Paul wrote to the believers at Corinth, "Ye are our epistle written in our hearts, known and read of all men: Forasmuch as ye are manifestly declared to be the epistle of Christ ministered by us, written not with ink, but with the Spirit of the living God; not in tables of stone, but in fleshy tables of the heart."

Like it or not, we are in the arena of the battle. We are on display. The world is watching. Satan will daily release the lions, prepare the stake, and light the fire. Can we win? Yes! Will we? That's going to depend on whether or not we have accessed the blood of the Lamb, guarded our testimony, and made a commitment to be faithful to the end.

> *Fear none of those things which thou shalt suffer: behold, the devil shall cast some of you into prison, that ye may be tried; and ye shall have tribulation ten days: be thou faithful unto death, and I will give thee a crown of life.*—REVELATION 2:10

CHAPTER THREE

Wicked Fire

Americans pride themselves in their right to bear arms. Second amendment controversies seem to be in the news on a regular basis. In 2012, 270 million guns were legally registered to private citizens in the United States. That would be nine guns for every ten people. Americans, however, are not the most armed people in the world. The country of Yemen has 20 million people and 50 million guns. The least armed country in the world is Nigeria. The largest private arsenal, however, is owned by the prince and power of this world—Satan himself.

Ephesians 6:16 identifies these weapons as "fiery darts." The metaphor here of "ignited darts" is taken from ancient warfare. The Roman *malleoli* were arrows with a bulb just below the point that was filled with burning liquid. These arrows were shot from a slack bow so that the fire would not be extinguished in route. The devil's arsenal is not designed with the intent upon killing you on impact, but rather injecting into your mind and heart poisonous, polluted, and perverted ideas and philosophies that will cause a slow but painful spiritual death.

Would you admit that you've been hit by one of these darts? What poison has been injected into your thinking, attitude, or behavior? The devil prepares his darts with bulbs filled with burning lust, pride, or bitterness and sends them daily in our direction. When they hit their target, they set on fire the course of nature. The human and sinful passions within each of us are ignited, and the damage is done. Let's look at three particular aspects of this arsenal that is launched against us on a daily basis.

YOU ARE THE TARGET

A dart or arrow is designed to hit a particular target. The devil doesn't use a shotgun and fire it at will hoping that he hits something. He has his scope dialed in on a particular area of our lives.

Several years ago, I was holding a revival in Cortez, Colorado. It was hunting season and a man in the church by the name of Steve Chappell (Pastor Paul Chappell's uncle) is an avid outdoorsman. His ranch, which he and his son farm, is located in an area where elk and deer are plentiful. Steve loves to guide men on a hunt for these magnificent animals. It was elk season while I was there, and on Sunday morning at church I met a man who had come to Cortez some twenty-five times to hunt on the ranch. He was an insurance man from the Los Angeles area, and I was delighted to learn that Steve had led him to Christ on one of his previous hunts a few years earlier.

They informed me that they had already been out early that Sunday morning and had spotted several herds and some good looking bull elk. I could tell that both this man and Steve were excited about the prospects of bringing down a prize trophy that week. On Wednesday night after church, I spoke to the man again and asked him if he had gotten his elk. With a proud smile he answered in the affirmative and in fact was returning to Los Angeles the following morning—his hunt successful. I asked him about the elk that he got, and while I could tell that he was pleased, it was evident that it was not the biggest or best he had ever brought down.

Later, I saw Steve and congratulated him on guiding a successful hunt. He looked at me disappointed and said, "Oh, it was such a shame."

"Why, what happened?"

Steve began to tell me how the day before they had spotted a beautiful bull elk just as the sun came up. The elk was massive and had a perfect rack—not one tip was chipped or broken. Steve told me how he positioned his friend carefully about one hundred yards away for the perfect shot. As his friend looked through the scope in the direction of the target, he whispered over his shoulder, "I don't see him." Steve couldn't believe his ears. The animal was standing in perfect view. He bent down and with his hands guided the man's head so as to put him in perfect line with the animal. But he still claimed, "I don't see him." The elk in those nervous moments looked in the hunter's direction, snorted, and moved behind some brush never to be seen again!

Steve, a little beyond upset, grabbed the man's gun and looked through the scope. Somehow in transporting that gun to the location, the dial had been moved—it was completely out of focus. The chance for the kill of a lifetime—lost!

Can I tell you that Satan's equipment is never outdated, out of focus, or in ill repair? He has his scope dialed in on you and has perfect aim. He is simply waiting for the perfect opportunity to pull the trigger and bring you down. As the devil walks up and down upon the earth seeking whom he may devour, what is he looking for?

Weakened Targets

The metaphor that the Holy Spirit chose to characterize Satan in 1 Peter 5:8 is "a roaring lion." Now I wouldn't claim to know a whole lot about lions, but in doing a bit of reading and watching a documentary or two, it would seem obvious to me that a lion, when hungry, does not go after the strongest in the herd. He crouches in the grass waiting for the one animal in the herd who strays from the others, or appears to be injured, or perhaps is young and not as savvy to the lion's tactics.

Weaknesses in our character make us vulnerable to the fiery darts in the devil's arsenal. All of us, if we are honest, can identify that weakness—that "sin that doth so easily beset us." Perhaps for Cain that weakness was jealousy. For Achan it was covetousness. Samson constantly battled his lust. King Saul fell because of pride. Peter succumbed to impatience more than once. Thomas is known as the doubting disciple. Martha was vulnerable to busyness. Demas had a problem with the attractions of this world. You can be sure that the devil has done his homework. He has his imps constantly scouting the target, and when he gets ready to fire, he will zero in on your ingrained weakness.

We must deal with these vulnerable areas. The writer of Hebrews tells us to "lay aside every weight, and the sin which doth so easily beset us" (Hebrews 12:1). No temptation is beyond victory. "There hath no temptation taken you but such as is common to man: but God is faithful, who will not suffer you to be tempted above that ye are able; but will with the temptation also make a way to escape, that ye may be able to bear it" (1 Corinthians 10:13). Confess and forsake that sin! Don't give Satan an easy target.

Wounded Targets

Have you ever been hurt? Sometime in life all of us suffer an injury. Somebody lets us down. Something is said. Something hurtful is done. We've gotten burned or stabbed in the back. Words and actions can hurt and leave a wound that doesn't heal quickly—at least not on its own. Satan sees these open wounds and sets his scope right on them. He fires dart after dart into the raw, unprotected wound and is able to ignite within us the passions of anger, bitterness, and revenge.

When we are wounded, we often feel justified in getting even. Our natural instinct is to treat that person the exact way he has treated us. We say to ourselves, "I'm going to give them a little of their own medicine!" But God has something to say about that: "Say not thou, I will recompense evil; but wait on the LORD, and he shall save thee" (Proverbs 20:22).

When the poison of that fiery dart spills out and fuels bitterness and revenge, we are in trouble. The Holy Spirit is grieved in our lives. This is why Ephesians 4:30–32 instructs, "And grieve not the holy Spirit of God, whereby ye are sealed unto the day of redemption. Let all bitterness, and wrath, and anger, and clamour, and evil speaking, be put away from you, with all malice: And be ye kind one to another, tenderhearted, forgiving one another, even as God for Christ sake hath forgiven you."

We have been forgiven by God, therefore we can forgive others! We may think we have a right to get even, but that attitude plays right into the devils hands. James 3:14–15 tells us, "But if ye have bitter envying and strife in your hearts, glory not, and lie not against the truth. This wisdom descendeth not from above, but is earthly, sensual, devilish."

We must close the wound caused by others. We are allowed to kill—but only with kindness and forgiveness.

Dearly beloved, avenge not yourselves, but rather give place unto wrath: for it is written, Vengeance is mine; I will repay, saith the Lord. Therefore if thine enemy hunger, feed him; if he thirst, give him drink: for in so doing thou shalt heap coals of fire on his head. Be

not overcome of evil, but overcome evil with good.
—ROMANS 12:19–21

When Jesus was cruelly beaten, scourged, crowned with thorns, spat upon, mocked, jeered, and nailed to a wooden cross, His response was, "Father, forgive them; for they know not what they do" (Luke 23:34). When Stephen was martyred for his testimony of faith, power, and good works, his response was: "Lord, lay not this sin to their charge" (Acts 7:60). With God's enablement we, too, can close the injurious wounds opened by others lest Satan have an advantage over us.

Inconsistent Targets

Had we been one of the twelve disciples, I think we would have admired about ninety five percent of Peter's life. He was bold, aggressive, energetic, and visionary. But he had his moments of inconsistency, and it was in those moments that he would fall prey to the wicked one.

Our Christian lives are often pictured in Scripture as a walk. Walking is one of the most basic and regular things that we do. While everyone has a different pace or gait to his walk, everyone has a certain consistency to his walk. God desires that we consistently imitate Him in our walk.

> *He that saith he abideth in him ought himself also so to walk, even as he walked.*—1 JOHN 2:6

> *As ye have therefore received Christ Jesus the Lord, so walk ye in him.*—COLOSSIANS 2:6

Too often our "pace" is different than God's.

God's Pace	Our Pace
Walk in newness of life —Romans 6:4	Walk after the old life
Walk honestly—Romans 13:13	Walk dishonestly
Walk by faith —2 Corinthians 5:7	Walk in doubt
Walk in the Spirit —Galatians 5:16	Walk in the flesh
Walk in good works —Ephesians 2:10	Walk in evil deeds
Walk in love—Ephesians 5:2	Walk in hatred
Walk as children of light —Ephesians 5:8	Walk as children of darkness
Walk circumspectly —Ephesians 5:15	Walk casually
Walk worthy of the Lord —Colossians 1:10	Walk like a child of the devil
Walk in wisdom —Colossians 4:5	Walk foolishly
Walk after His commandments—2 John 6	Walk in rebellion

When we walk contrary to God's pace, we have a dart headed our way! We may not believe this to be the case—Peter didn't. But, just as in Peter's case, it is true nonetheless. Before

Peter denied the Lord, Jesus warned him of his weakness, but Peter wouldn't hear of it.

> *And the Lord said, Simon, Simon, behold, Satan hath desired to have you, that he may sift you as wheat: But I have prayed for thee, that thy faith fail not: and when thou are converted, strengthen thy brethren. And he said unto him, Lord, I am ready to go with thee, both into prison, and to death. And he said, I tell thee, Peter, the cock shall not crow this day, before that thou shalt thrice deny that thou knowest me—*LUKE 22:31–34

Only twenty-two verses later we read how accurate Christ was:

> *And when they had kindled a fire in the midst of the hall, and were set down together, Peter sat down among them. But a certain maid beheld him as he sat by the fire, and earnestly looked upon him, and said, This man was also with him. And he denied him, saying, Woman, I know him not. And after a little while another saw him, and said, Thou art also of them. And Peter said, Man, I am not. And about the space of one hour after another confidently affirmed, saying, Of a truth this fellow also was with him: or he is a Galilaean. And Peter said, Man, I know not what thou sayest. And immediately, while he yet spake, the cock crew. And the Lord turned, and looked upon Peter. And Peter remembered the word of the Lord, how he had said unto him, Before the cock crow,*

thou shalt deny me thrice. And Peter went out, and wept
bitterly.—LUKE 22:55–62

An inconsistent walk makes us a sure target.

Unguarded Targets

The older you get the easier it is to gain weight. Spiritually, if we are not careful, we are also prone to lug around some extra pounds as we journey through life. It might be the burden of an unsaved or wayward loved one. It could be a physical illness or financial uncertainty. A broken marriage or the loss of employment can be an incredible burden. These burdens make us easy targets for the fiery darts of the wicked one.

You see, we only have two hands, and God has commanded us in Ephesians 6 to take the shield of faith in one hand and the sword of the Spirit in the other. That doesn't leave any hands to pick up a burden. When we do, we must put down our shield and our sword. To discard the shield and sword leaves us unprotected. And so, God commands us to "lay aside every weight" (Hebrews 12:1). In 1 Peter 5:7, He invites us to cast "all your care upon him; for he careth for you."

Incidentally, isn't it interesting that the next verse says, "Be sober, be vigilant; because your adversary the devil, as a roaring lion, walketh about, seeking whom he may devour"? He is definitely seeking out those who are carrying a weight that should have been given to the "Burden Bearer!"[1]

---

1   For a great read on this subject, *The Burden Bearer* by Dr. Paul Chappell
     (Striving Together Publications, 2012) will greatly help and encourage you.

God is capable of handling your cares of life, and Jesus told His disciples to let Him do it without the intervention of worry:

*Therefore I say unto you, Take no thought for your life, what ye shall eat, or what ye shall drink; nor yet for your body, what ye shall put on. Is not the life more than meat, and the body than raiment? Behold the fowls of the air: for they sow not, neither do they reap, nor gather into barns; yet your heavenly Father feedeth them. Are ye not much better than they? Which of you by taking thought can add one cubit unto his stature? And why take ye thought for raiment? Consider the lilies of the field, how they grow; they toil not, neither do they spin: And yet I say unto you, That even Solomon in all his glory was not arrayed like one of these. Wherefore, if God so clothe the grass of the field, which to day is, and to morrow is cast into the oven, shall he not much more clothe you, O ye of little faith? Therefore take no thought, saying, What shall we eat? or, What shall we drink? or, Wherewithal shall we be clothed? (For after all these things do the Gentiles seek:) for your heavenly Father knoweth that ye have need of all these things. But seek ye first the kingdom of God, and his righteousness; and all these things shall be added unto you.—*MATTHEW 6:25–33

If when the devil sets his scope on you, he cannot see a weakness, wound, inconsistency, or unguarded heart, he has one more area he can target.

Insincere Targets

Satan saves some of his most proficient darts for the religious. He loves to trip up those who profess to be Christians, because a hypocrite is a great showpiece for Satan to use in the lives of those who are lost.

As we labor for the Lord, we must be careful not to allow our work to replace our worship. Our hands must never replace our heart nor our duties replace our devotion.

Martha was a woman who loved Jesus Christ dearly. The Lord was reciprocal in His love for Martha, her brother Lazarus, and their sister Mary. He would often come by their home in Bethany to visit these good friends.

On one occasion, it appears that Christ's coming was announced in advance because Martha was doing everything possible to prepare for this special time. The day didn't go exactly as she had planned, however.

> *Now it came to pass, as they went, that he entered into a certain village: and a certain woman named Martha received him into her house. And she had a sister called Mary, which also sat at Jesus' feet, and heard his word. But Martha was cumbered about much serving, and came to him, and said, Lord, dost thou not care that my sister hath left me to serve alone? bid her therefore*

that she help me. And Jesus answered and said unto her, Martha, Martha, thou art careful and troubled about many things: But one thing is needful: and Mary hath chosen that good part, which shall not be taken away from her.—LUKE 10:38–42

Martha meant well, and I believe that her motives were sincere. But with the Lord, the outer never replaces the inner. The Lord identified this problem back in Isaiah's day: "Wherefore the Lord said, Forasmuch as this people draw near me with their mouth, and with their lips do honour me, but have removed their heart far from me, and their fear toward me is taught by the precept of men" (Isaiah 29:13). Too often we are concerned only with what men think of our work while God is gazing deeply into our hearts.

For instance, how many picture frames do you have hanging on the wall of your home or sitting on the shelves without pictures in them? I seriously doubt that you have any! Now I would guess you have a few pictures in a drawer or a scrap book without frames. What's important? The picture or the frame? It's not a trick question—the picture is what is important—the frame only enhances the picture on the inside. Yet so often we are content "having a form of godliness, but denying the power thereof" (2 Timothy 3:5). We have a form—we go to church, in fact, we are members. We carry the right Bible, sing the right songs, pray the right prayers, give the right testimonies, but the inside is empty. We have constructed beautiful frames but have let Satan confiscate the picture! When we lose the power of God, we will lose the war.

Satan's weapons are in good repair. He has them lined up and aimed in our direction. His scope is dialed in on a particular target.

A PARALYZING TACTIC

Ephesians 6:16 identifies Satan's arsenal as "fiery darts." Fire has a paralyzing effect.

When I was a boy, my father was the caretaker of a cemetery about three miles from our farm. Once a week during the spring, summer, and fall, our family would go to the cemetery and mow the grass, water the flowers, and provide any other needed upkeep. When someone would die, my dad and uncle would dig the grave. I well remember helping them dig my grandfather's grave.

At age thirteen, I went to my dad and inquired about the possibility of taking over his job as caretaker. I was raising rabbits at the time and would sell them for sixteen cents a pound. I wasn't getting to my first million very fast! I needed a real job. Sure enough, the cemetery board agreed that I could handle the responsibilities, so for the next five years I mowed grass and dug graves at the River Road Cemetery. I received ten dollars each time I mowed and ten dollars for each grave I dug. (By the way, we didn't have riding lawn mowers. We didn't have self-propelled lawn mowers. We didn't even have lawnmowers with motors. We had the kind that the faster you pushed them, the faster the blades went around!)

One spring my Dad suggested that we go over together and clean out the fence line on the south end of the cemetery. It was entangled with brush and thorns, and getting them pulled out early in the spring would be much easier than later on when they started growing again. We worked all day to get the job done and had a huge pile of brush across the road in a vacant lot. It was time for the evening chores, and Dad, who was heading home to get started, told me to go to the equipment shed and get some matches and gasoline and burn the pile of brush before I came home.

I was ecstatic! That pile of brush was twenty feet high and as big around as a softball diamond. This was going to be fun. I retrieved the matches and a five gallon can of gasoline filled to the top. I had watched my Dad do this kind of stuff before, so I was cautious as I began sprinkling a few drops of gasoline around the edge of that brush pile. I struck a match and threw it in ready to back-pedal as I did.

To my disappointment, nothing happened. I thought—"it needs more gasoline." I grabbed the can and splashed more of the liquid around the edges and again struck a match—but to my dismay—nothing happened.

I decided that what I needed to do was get a small fire burning and then add gasoline. I got a few small twigs, broke them up, and pushed them into the pile. I carefully got them burning just a bit and went back for the gas. I took the can and, with the lid open, hurled that liquid in the direction of the small flames.

The next few seconds are a bit foggy in my memory. I remember seeing fire coming toward me following the gasses of the liquid spewing from the can. Before it reached me I threw the gas can as high as I could over my head and began to run for the other side of the road! The gas can exploded overhead and landed into the brush pile now roaring with fire. The next few moments were some of the scariest of my life as flames soared and the sky was blackened by thick smoke while I stood motionless across the road thinking I had just set the world on fire!

I can tell you from experience that fire has a paralyzing effect. I see two reasons why Satan would add fire to his arsenal of darts.

To Distract Us

Whenever there is a fire out of control like that day at the cemetery, the only thought that occupies our minds is getting that fire out. My only focus in those next moments was a fire focus. Nothing else mattered!

Likewise, once Satan's dart successfully hits its target, the fire ignites, and now our only focus in life is on that fire. For instance, I have counseled many people over the years who were struggling with assurance of salvation. It is impossible for them to grow or be fruitful because the fire of doubt has overtaken them.

When a Christian allows sin in his life and refuses to deal with it, his only concern is that no one will find out. He doesn't get anything out of his Bible reading, his prayers hit the ceiling and bounce back, his worship seems hollow, and no one seems interested in his testimony. He is paralyzed in his Christian life by the continuous distraction of sin. This is all part of Satan's strategy in using "fiery darts."

To Confuse Us

When a fire is out of control we are never sure what to do. A thousand thoughts may go through our minds, but our feet can't decide in which direction to run.

My oldest son, John, was engaged to be married and during a break from college wanted to drive two hundred miles to Fresno, California, to help his fiancé, April, with some wedding planning. I was fine with his going, but he wanted to take my car since his wasn't that reliable. I had a Geo Prism at the time and absolutely loved that little car. Reluctantly, I let him borrow it.

One day while in Fresno he was driving down Highway 99 with April and two of her siblings. In front of him was an old pick-up truck carrying a load of junk including a box spring mattress tied to the very top of the heap. Suddenly, the mattress came loose and landed in the middle lane of traffic in which John was driving. Quickly looking to his right and left and seeing cars beside him, he chose to try to straddle the mattress at sixty miles an hour. It didn't work. Some of the springs from the mattress got up into his engine and immediately started a fire. He was able to quickly maneuver the car to the shoulder of the road, but by now the engine was engulfed in flames. Fortunately, the four of them managed to escape the car.

When I asked John later what he did at that point, his response was, "I didn't know what to do." Actually, his fiancé jumped a wire fence and ran to a fire station that just so happened to be on the frontage road near the mishap. By the time the firefighters arrived, there wasn't much left of my Prism. Like Adam and Eve, when the fiery dart hits, we often hide, run, cover, or blame shift. We are confused and never think to confess.

I'll address this further in the next chapter when we get to the armor, but this is why it is so important that we have our "shield of faith." This shield is the only defense we have to extinguish these ignited darts. For now, notice these verses that speak to the importance of our shield of faith:

> *For whatsoever is born of God overcometh the world: and this is the victory that overcometh the world, even our faith.*—1 JOHN 5:4

> *But let us, who are of the day, be sober, putting on the breastplate of faith and love; and for an helmet, the hope of salvation.*—1 THESSALONIANS 5:8

> *Holding faith, and a good conscience; which some having put away concerning faith have made shipwreck.*
> —1 TIMOTHY 1:19

> *Fight the good fight of faith…*—1 TIMOTHY 6:12

Let us draw near with a true heart in full assurance of faith…—HEBREWS 10:22

The arsenal of Satan is dialed in on a particular target and is designed to have a paralyzing effect. But there is one more element to his weapons. Remember the Roman *malleoli?* There was a bulb of burning liquid just beneath the tip of the dart that was poisonous in nature. The dart itself was not designed to kill, but the liquid poison entering the body would indeed over time take the life of the victim.

THOUGHT POLLUTION

The devil loves to inject a poisonous venom into our attitudes, thinking, and philosophy that will in time take us in the opposite direction from God and will ultimately destroy us. Satan destroys from the inside out, and once he gets the poison into our thinking, the destructive actions will follow. Proverbs 23:7 observes, "For as he thinketh in his heart, so is he." This is why Scripture warns, "Keep thy heart with all diligence; for out of it are the issues of life" (Proverbs 4:23).

We know Satan's goal, but how do we keep his poison out?

Close the Gates

There are only two ways that something can enter our brains. I used to think when I was in school that if I placed my textbook under my pillow and slept with my head on the pillow directly over the textbook, that through some kind of osmosis the information in the book would diffuse into my brain and I would be able to pass the test the next day. I have put that theory to the test and proved it wrong on several occasions. It would be nice if there was an app on our cell phone called "the brain app" which we could program with Bible verses and principles and then access it when we needed them.

The only two entry points into our mind are the eyes and the ears. Unfortunately, we often leave them unguarded. Jesus warned in Matthew 6:22–23, "The light of the body is the eye: if therefore thine eye be single, thy whole body shall be full of light. But if thine eye be evil, thy whole body shall be full of darkness. If therefore the light that is in thee be darkness, how great is that darkness!" This is why the Psalmist said, "I will set no wicked thing before mine eyes" (Psalm 101:3). Jeremiah said, "Mine eye affecteth mine heart" (Lamentations 3:51).

Do you remember the Old Testament character by the name of Lot? He was Abraham's nephew. According to Genesis 13, both Abraham and Lot had a large number of cattle along with servants to care for them. But a controversy arose between them, and from there it led to a bad decision. Listen to the details:

> *And the land was not able to bear them, that they might dwell together: for their substance was great, so that they could not dwell together. And there was a strife between the herdmen of Abram's cattle and the herdman of Lot's cattle: and the Canaanite and the Perizzite dwelled then in the land. And Abram said unto Lot, Let there be*

no strife, I pray thee, between me and thee, and between my herdmen and thy herdmen; for we be brethren. Is not the whole land before thee? separate thyself, I pray thee, from me: if thou wilt take the left hand, then I will go to the right; or if thou depart to the right hand, then I will go to the left.—GENESIS 13:6–9

Now before we read the rest of the story; have you ever wondered what would have happened to Abraham if Lot had chosen the proper direction? He is given a choice between the right hand and the left. Now we know, or will soon find out, that Lot chose the wrong direction and ended up in Sodom. But what if he had chosen the proper way? Would that mean that Abraham would have ended up in Sodom? Think carefully through the rest of the passage:

And Lot lifted up his eyes, and beheld all the plain of Jordan, that it was well watered every where, before the LORD destroyed Sodom and Gomorrah, even as the garden of the LORD, like the land of Egypt, as thou comest unto Zoar. Then Lot chose him all the plain of Jordan; and Lot journeyed east: and they separated themselves the one from the other. Abram dwelled in the land of Canaan, and Lot dwelled in the cities of the plain, and pitched his tent toward Sodom. But the men of Sodom were wicked and sinners before the LORD exceedingly.—GENESIS 13:10–13

Lot didn't choose right or left. He lifted up his eyes, saw the plains of Jordan and walked east right into Sodom! But while I'm not going to cut Lot any slack here; he should have listened to his elder and heeded his counsel, I don't see that Lot was a wicked man at this point of a wrong decision. He most certainly was not the derelict he was at the end of his life when he is up in a cave drunk and committing incest with his two daughters. (See Genesis 19:30–38.) So how did Lot go from making a simple wrong decision to becoming intoxicated enough to father two sons of his own daughters who would become leaders of God-hating idolatrous nations?

We would never guess that Lot was a believer from reading the accounts in Genesis. But in 2 Peter, God calls him both *just* and *righteous*. These terms speak of his position rather than his practice. But notice the key to his downfall and ours if we leave the gates to our minds unguarded: "And delivered just Lot, vexed with the filthy conversation of the wicked: (For that righteous man dwelling among them, *in seeing and hearing,* vexed his righteous soul from day to day with their unlawful deeds)" (2 Peter 2:7–8).

Seeing and hearing! The eyes and the ears! The two entry points into the brain became conduits for the filth of Sodom. No wonder Lot's soul was vexed, his family destroyed, and his own life devoured by Satan!

What are you looking at with your eyes and listening to with your ears? Have you built in any safeguards or accountability? With today's technology, sin is at our fingertips in the form of our phones, iPads, computers, and a whole lot more. All around us through light waves and air waves we are bombarded with poison from the wicked one. Close the gate or suffer the fate!

Arrest Intruders

Now let's be honest at this point. No matter how well we protect our eyes and our ears, there are times when Satan maneuvers a poisonous dart right past the guards. It might be a billboard on the side of the road that poisons our minds with a lustful thoughts or a critical word from a co-worker that causes anger. It might be an unanswered (at least in our minds) prayer request that produces doubt, or an unexpected expense that brings on worry. As we have noted, once inside this poison is designed to destroy. So what should be our response when the devil successfully slips in some poison?

Second Corinthians 10:5 tells us plainly: "Casting down imaginations, and every high thing that exalteth itself against the knowledge of God, and bringing into captivity every thought to the obedience of Christ." I would argue that all of us know when something has entered our thinking that is contrary to the "knowledge of God." God has written His law on our hearts and consciences. Romans 2:15 says, "Which shew the work of the law written in their hearts, their conscience also bearing witness, and their thoughts the mean while accusing or else excusing one another." What thought is in your mind that God would not think? Why is it there? God tells us to immediately cast it down and handcuff it—like a policeman who in hot pursuit of a criminal does not let up until that offender is caught, tackled, and cuffed.

The old thought once under arrest must be replaced by the right thought.[2] Ephesians 4:22–24 instructs, "That ye put off concerning the former conversation the old man, which is corrupt according to the deceitful lusts; And be renewed in the spirit of your mind; And that ye put on the new man, which after God is created in righteousness and true holiness." We must put off the deceitful lustful thoughts—the old man thinking, and replace it with righteous and holy thoughts—the new man thinking.

Failure to challenge the exalted wrong thoughts that enter our mind will bring about our downfall. An old mind will defeat a new man every time! If you are saved, you are a new creature in Christ, but if you don't do something about the old creature thoughts, they will destroy the new creature testimony every time. When poisonous thoughts are left to roam free in our minds, they will find their way into disastrous actions.

IT COULD HAPPEN TO YOU

You will act out what you think on. Matthew 15:18–20 tells us that mind eventually becomes manner: "But those things which proceed out of the mouth come forth from the heart; and they defile the man. For out of the heart proceed evil

---

2   For a more detailed look at this principle, see my book entitled *What's on Your Mind?* (Striving Together Publications, 2008).

thoughts, murders, adulteries, fornications, thefts, false witness, blasphemies: These are the things which defile a man...."

Think of it: Satan's goal is that everyone reading these pages will commit murder, adultery, fornication, theft, false witness, and blasphemy! How would he possibly accomplish that? He will take a dart and aim it at our weaknesses, wounds, inconsistencies, unguarded places, or insincerities in our worship. He will put some fire with that dart to continuously distract you and confuse your direction. He will then add some poison and shoot that dart through an unguarded entrance. Once inside he will exalt that sin above any resistance so that in time the expression will be murder, adultery, fornication, theft, false witness, and blasphemy.

Don't think it can happen? Oh, it does! Years ago I heard Dr. Tom Wallace tell the story about a young man in his church by the name of David. Almost as soon as he was saved, he had a desire to serve the Lord. He came to his pastor one day and asked him if there was some ministry in the church in which he could serve. Dr. Wallace mentioned that the church had a bus ministry, and if David would like he could come the following Saturday, he would pair him up with one of the captains and he could go out and invite folks to ride on the bus.

David was overjoyed at this prospect of having a part in weekly ministry in his local church. He came that next Saturday and visited in the neighborhoods with the bus captain and the following day rode the bus and helped bring in the old and new riders. The bus route grew with his help and soon the captain went to the pastor and asked for a second bus. Soon that bus was filled with riders. The captain approached his pastor and said, "Pastor, that young man you gave me for my bus route is killing me. He is dynamite but I can't handle any more bus kids. Get that guy his own bus and a driver. I guarantee you he will fill a bus!"

The church bought another bus and engaged a driver. David now had his own bus route and was bringing people to Christ through his ministry every week. David was in the Army, stationed at a nearby base, and had a particular burden for military men. Throughout the week he would invite soldiers to ride his bus on Sunday. His pastor reported that there was rarely a Sunday when two or three servicemen did not walk the aisle and trust Christ because of this young man's testimony and ministry.

One Sunday night, as his pastor was preaching, David heard something with which he wasn't sure if he agreed. Like a dart it entered his mind, and he couldn't escape it. Rather than go to his pastor as he should have after the service, he went home with this poison. Over the next days it bothered him more and more, and now when he would sit in church, it seemed that everything his pastor was preaching was contrary to his thinking. Soon David quit attending on Wednesday nights and shortly after gave up his bus route. His pastor, fellow bus workers, and friends confronted David to try to help him, but David pushed them aside saying it was nothing—just something he needed to deal with.

It wasn't long until he stopped attending on Sunday night and a few weeks later quit church altogether. Again, many tried to help, but the poison was now affecting his mind and his manner. After he was discharged from the Army, he decided to leave Louisville, Kentucky. He was tired of these church people bugging him about getting right with God and coming back to church. To get as far away from the church as possible, he moved to the city of New York. No one would know him there. He was free to live as he chose.

To make a long story short, David still resides in the state of New York. He will do so for the rest of his life. You see, David Berkewitz is not known to Americans by that name. He is known as the "Son of Sam." As a young man he murdered several young ladies in cold blood. His parole has come up for the final time and he has been refused. The rest of his life will be spent behind bars.

When my son, Brock, was preparing for his senior speech recital, he asked me if he could do it on the story of the Son of Sam. With my permission, he wrote David in prison and received a letter in response. David is doing his best to live for Jesus Christ while incarcerated. He reads his Bible and tries to witness to his fellow inmates. He gave Brock permission to tell his story but pleaded with him to remind people that sin starts with something very small and seemingly harmless.

Satan's arsenal consists of "fiery darts." As we said in the beginning of this chapter, the dart is not designed to kill you. But that dart is fueled with a burning poisonous liquid and once the dart successfully hits its mark, the wound is opened and the poison enters. A slow painful death follows.

Suppose, as you were reading this book your phone rang. It was the police department in your town. The officer on the other end confirmed your address and then informed you that a sniper was positioned across the street from your house atop a building nearby. The police have been in contact with him and he is intent on shooting anyone who exits your front door. He is armed with a high powered rifle with a sophisticated scope and presently has it aimed at your front entrance. What would you do? Would you dismiss the call as a joke, walk to the front door, open it, and step out on your porch? You would be an absolute fool! You'd listen to every word of that police officer and do exactly what he told you to do.

So what are you going to do now that you know we have an enemy far more armed and dangerous than any human sniper? I suggest you read on—God has provided the protection we need. Ephesians 6 provides a warning, but it's also about winning! It's time to put on some armor!

CHAPTER FOUR

Provision for Victory

Early in our marriage, my wife and I lived in West Virginia. The village where we lived (Smithburg) had two buildings—our house and the county highway garage next door. I was just getting started in revival work in those days and so would be gone for three or four weeks and then be home for three or four days before heading out again. The house was old, and it seemed there was always something to fix during my days home. The yard, too, was in constant need of attention.

I had gotten to know a few of the men who worked for the county as they would come by the garage to pick up equipment or eat their lunch.

One day as I was working in the yard, one of those men called to me: "John! Have you ever seen a copperhead snake?"

"No," I quickly answered.

"Would you like to see one?"

I responded with the only sensible question, "Dead or alive?"

He said it was dead, but knowing these guys enough to know their penchant for practical jokes, I approached cautiously. He was looking at the ground as I walked up and pointing near his feet. I didn't see anything at first and so asked, "Where is it?" He knelt down and picked up a small snake about twenty inches long. It didn't look all that impressive, especially since it was missing its head!

When I enquired about the head, he said, "John, you don't want to be anywhere near one of these, dead or alive, if they still have their heads. There is venom in the head of these snakes that can kill you even after it's been chopped off." I was thankful he had already buried the head and was grateful for the information.

When I asked where he found the snake, his eyes could have bored a hole through me as he pointed to the county shed to the right of us. "They've made their nests in those sand piles inside that building; I bet there are a thousand of them in there!"

That building was five feet from our property line! I had mowed the grass alongside that building dozens of times. I never saw another copperhead in the six months we lived there, but I was surely looking for them.

Between the fall of man and the final judgment, there is a lot of the serpent bruising the heel of Jesus Christ. Shortly after the fall of man in the Garden of Eden, God had some stern words for the serpent, but He included in them a wonderful promise: "And I will put enmity between thee and the woman, and between thy seed and her seed; it shall bruise thy head, and thou shalt bruise his heel" (Genesis 3:15). One day, Satan's head will be crushed as he is finally defeated and cast into Hell. As for now, however, he still has his head and he slithers about us each and every day ready to inject his poisonous venom into our lives.

Can we have victory over this enemy? The disciples knew that they were up against a formidable enemy as they ministered during the time of Christ. They were just ordinary men being asked to confront a wicked generation with the truth of the gospel. Jesus understood their fears and gave them a promise in Luke 10:19: "Behold, I give you power to tread on serpents and scorpions, and over all the power of the enemy: and nothing shall by any means hurt you."

This victory is not in or of ourselves—it is only possible through the Lord Jesus Christ. "But thanks be to God, which giveth us the victory through our Lord Jesus Christ" (1 Corinthians 15:57).

Every child of God ought to memorize and revel daily in these words that assure us a victory:

> *Who shall separate us from the love of Christ? shall tribulation, or distress, or persecution, or famine, or nakedness, or peril, or sword? As it is written, For thy sake we are killed all the day long; we are accounted as sheep for the slaughter. Nay, in all these things we are more than conquerors through him that loved us. For I am persuaded, that neither death, nor life, nor angels,*

nor principalities, nor powers, nor things present, nor things to come, Nor height, nor depth, nor any other creature, shall be able to separate us from the love of God, which is in Christ Jesus our Lord.—ROMANS 8:35–39

In this chapter, we will consider vital components to the victory we can claim as we see the armor God has given us.

GOD'S PROVISION OF GRACE

Outside of Christ, we are no match for this enemy. The victory is only possible "through him that loved us" (Romans 8:37). "Not that we are sufficient of ourselves to think any thing as of ourselves; but our sufficiency is of God" (2 Corinthians 3:5). We can do all things, but only through Christ which strengthens us. (See Philippians 4:13.)

ACCESS TO GOD'S GRACE

The introductory part of any passage of Scripture is extremely important, and Ephesians 6, as the apostle is about to inform us of our armor for the battle, is no different. He begins with the words, "Finally, my brethren" (verse 10). "Brother" or "brethren" may be an unfamiliar term to some, but among believers in Christ it signifies our identification in the family of God. People on the other side of the planet are our brothers and sisters because of our relationship with Jesus Christ. "But as many as received him, to them gave he power to become he sons of God, even to them that believe on his name" (John 1:12).

Most important to victory, however, is not our relationship to each other, but our relationship to Jesus Christ. We looked at this in chapter 1, but it is so foundational to our ability to use the armor of God that we will look at it once again here. To access God's grace we must first be the children of God! No one is born with this relationship; it must be established. Jesus told Nicodemus, "Except a man be born again, he cannot see the kingdom of God. …Ye must be born again" (John 3:3, 7). Nicodemus was confused. He wondered how he, as a grown man, could return to his mother's womb and experience birth again. Jesus, however, was speaking of a new birth—a spiritual birth.

Physical birth and spiritual birth both take place at an exact moment. Your birth certificate has a time and a date stamped on it proving when you came into this world. Has there been a specific time and place when you trusted Christ as your Saviour?

This relationship is not established when we join a church, get baptized, or experience some kind of reformation. Those are all things we can do, and the Bible is clear that we cannot save ourselves from our sin.

> Not by works of righteousness which we have done, but according to his mercy he saved us, by the washing of regeneration, and renewing of the Holy Ghost; Which he shed on us abundantly through Jesus Christ our Saviour.—TITUS 3:5–6

For by grace are ye saved through faith; and that not of yourselves: it is the gift of God: Not of works, lest any man should boast.—EPHESIANS 2:8–9

We are born physically on the wrong side. "Behold, I was shapen in iniquity; and in sin did my mother conceive me" (Psalm 51:5). Our sin nature then leads us down a path of sin. This is why we must be born again!

And you hath he quickened, who were dead in trespasses and sins; Wherein in time past ye walked according to the course of this world, according to the prince of the power of the air, the spirit that now worketh in the children of disobedience: Among whom also we all had our conversation in times past in the lust of our flesh, fulfilling the desires of the flesh and of the mind; and were by nature the children of wrath, even as others.
—EPHESIANS 2:1–3

When we turn from our sin and put our faith in Jesus Christ, a marvelous transformation takes place: "Therefore if any man be in Christ, he is a new creature: old things are passed away; behold, all things are become new" (2 Corinthians 5:17).

Do you have this divine relationship? Many people claim that they do, but remember that every relationship requires two people. I could say that my wife's name is Judy, but there is not a Judy in the world who would claim me as her husband! (My wife's name is Diane.) You can call yourself a Christian, but the real question is, *What does God call you?* Often times during an invitation time at the close of a message in church, the preacher will ask those who are born again to raise their hands as a testimony of that fact. The real question is not whether or not you will raise your hand. What matters is whether or not God would raise His hand acknowledging that you are a Christian. Romans 8:16 says that when we have been born again, "The Spirit itself beareth witness with our spirit, that we are the children of God." And if we have not been born again—"…if any man have not the Spirit of Christ, he is none of his" (Romans 8:9).

Jesus has some sobering words in regard to this matter.

Not every one that saith unto me, Lord, Lord, shall enter into the kingdom of heaven; but he that doeth the will of my Father which is in heaven. Many will say to me in that day, Lord, Lord, have we not prophesied in thy name? and in thy name cast out devils? and in thy name done many wonderful works? And then will I profess unto them, I never knew you: depart from me, ye that work iniquity.—MATTHEW 7:21–23

We find a similar warning in the gospel of Luke:

Strive to enter in at the strait gate: for many, I say unto you, will seek to enter in, and shall not be able. When once the master of the house is risen up, and hath shut to the door, and ye begin to stand without, and to knock at the door, saying, Lord, Lord, open unto us; and he shall answer and say unto you, I know you not whence ye are: Then shall ye begin to say, We have eaten and drunk in

thy presence, and thou hast taught in our streets. But
he shall say, I tell you, I know you not whence ye are:
depart from me, all ye workers of iniquity. There shall
be weeping and gnashing of teeth, when ye shall see
Abraham, and Isaac, and Jacob, and all the prophets,
in the kingdom of God, and you yourselves thrust out.
—LUKE 13:24–28

Make sure that you are in the faith! A divine relationship is absolutely essential to victory in spiritual warfare. If you don't have that relationship, God would have you trust Him as Saviour today. "For he saith, I have heard thee in a time accepted, and in the day of salvation have I succoured thee: behold, now is the accepted time; behold, now is the day of salvation" (2 Corinthians 6:2).

To be victorious in the spiritual battle, we need God's grace, and we access His grace by becoming His child.

POWER TO OVERCOME

Notice the rest of Ephesians 6:10: "Finally, my brethren, be strong in the Lord, and in the power of his might."

How are you going to win this war over Satan? In your strength? In your power?

Not on your life! Remember, this is not a battle against flesh and blood. We are up against Satan and all of his fallen angels. Do you need a reminder that these angels have supernatural power? (See Chapter 2 where one good angel wiped out 185,000 Assyrians overnight!)

We may have had some success in the past but we dare not get overconfident. First Corinthians 10:12 warns, "Wherefore let him that thinketh he standeth take heed lest he fall."

The ammunition to defeat our adversary is found only in the power of God. "Both riches and honour come of thee, and thou reignest over all; and in thine hand is power and might; and in thine hand it is to make great, and to give strength unto all" (1 Chronicles 29:12). "God hath spoken once; twice have I heard this; that power belongeth unto God" (Psalm 62:11).

READY EVERY DAY

Once the Apostle Paul reminds us of the foundation of victory— our relationship with Jesus Christ—and our source of power— the power of God—he begins the next verse with the words, "Put on" (Ephesians 6:11). This phrase indicates something that is to be done daily. I "put on" my shoes every day.

Readying ourselves for battle is not done once in a lifetime but rather every single day of our lives. Hit and miss Christianity is not going to produce victory in spiritual warfare. The psalmist wrote, "…that I may *daily* perform my vows" (Psalm 61:8). Proverbs 8:34 promises, "Blessed is the man that heareth me, watching *daily* at my gates, waiting at the posts of my doors." Jesus didn't redeem us to offer a "Sunday morning only" Christianity. True discipleship is daily discipleship. "And he said to them all, If any man will come after me, let him deny himself, and take up his cross daily, and follow me" (Luke 9:23).

We marvel at the courage of Joseph as he faithfully stands up to his master's wife: "And it came to pass after these things, that his master's wife cast her eyes upon Joseph; and she said, Lie with me. But he refused, and said unto his master's wife, Behold, my master wotteth not what is with me in the house, and he hath committed all that he hath to my hand; There is none greater in this house than I; neither hath he kept back any thing from me but thee, because thou art his wife: how then can I do this great wickedness, and sin against God?" (Genesis 39:7–9).

Joseph was all alone in Egypt and could have easily succumbed to the temptation of this no doubt beautiful woman. He could have reasoned that no one would ever find out. Being sold by his brothers into slavery could have provided an excuse to give up on God and follow his own fleshly desires. But he stood firm and true in the battle—and won!

Interestingly though, his first victory didn't mark the end of battle for him. Notice the next verse: "And it came to pass, as she spake to Joseph *day by day,* that he hearkened not unto her, to lie by her, or to be with her." The temptation didn't come just once but rather day after day after day.

I know this isn't the most glamorous or welcome news, but we are in this spiritual warfare for the rest of our earthly lives. There is no cease fire. No truce. No treaty. There may be seasons of less intensity, but the serpent still has his head! God has given us a provision of grace but we must access it every moment of every day.

STAND YOUR GROUND

God is about to equip us in Ephesians 6 with armor (we will get to the armor before the end of this chapter), but before He does, He tells us why we need it: "that ye may be able to stand against the wiles of the devil" (Ephesians 6:11).

The word *stand* has the connotation of "to fight" as no one fights very well sitting or lying down! But it also carries the idea of "holding one's ground." We might use the phrase "stand firm" or "stand your ground" and by doing so mean that we must hold on to territory that rightfully belongs to us.

As believers, we belong to Christ. We are His and we must not "give place to the devil" (Ephesians 4:27).

Once Satan gets a place in our lives, he can set up camp with a full array of artillery aimed in our direction. When a military unit first invades enemy territory, they must establish a place (a beachhead or foothold) to be in a position for victory. All Satan needs is a little ground in your life, and he will have an advantage in the battle. I believe this is what Paul is speaking of to the Corinthian believers in 2 Corinthians 2:11: "Lest Satan should get an advantage of us: for we are not ignorant of his devices."

One of the ways in which we must stand our ground is in our personal testimony. You and I bear the name of Christ! The word *Christian* means "Christ like." There is little that is more important than a good name or a good reputation.

*A good name is rather to be chosen than great
riches, and loving favour rather than silver and gold.*
—PROVERBS 22:1

A good name is better than a precious ointment....
—ECCLESIASTES 7:1

We must stand and fight for that good name. People around us aren't always listening, but they are always watching. "Ye are our epistle written in our hearts, known and read of all men: Forasmuch as ye are manifestly declared to be the epistle of Christ ministered by us, written not with ink, but with the Spirit of the living God; not in tables of stone, but in fleshy tables of the heart" (2 Corinthians 3:2).

We sometimes want to hide behind the verse that tells us God sees our hearts; but that same verse tells us that man looks on the outward appearance (1 Samuel 16:7).

We may not care about our testimonies or whether or not someone thinks good or ill of us, but the ramifications are so much bigger than us individually. How many people use the hypocrisy of a Christian they once knew to excuse themselves from their responsibility? The message of God is pointed here: "Giving no offence in anything, that the ministry be not blamed" (2 Corinthians 6:3). "It is good neither to eat flesh, nor to drink wine, nor any thing whereby thy brother stumbleth, or is offended, or is made weak" (Romans 14:21).

One day in Heaven we will meet people who are there because of an influence we had on their lives. Perhaps we prayed for them to be saved, handed them a gospel tract, gave money to print the tract, supported a missionary, or actually led them to Christ. In any case, they will be in Heaven because of us! But will there be anyone in Hell because of us? That is truly a sobering thought.

David committed a terrible sin with Bathsheba which led to all kinds of wrong doing, including murder! The judgment on David was severe, and I'm sure that he was reminded of his sin and the wages of it for the rest of his life. But there was a consequence beyond David and his immediate family. Nathan the prophet, after pronouncing the individual judgments that were to come, added: "Howbeit, because by this deed thou hast given great occasion to the enemies of the LORD to blaspheme…" (2 Samuel 12:14). People knew who David was—the sweet psalmist of Israel, the man after God's own heart, the king of God's chosen people—and they were laughing at God because David had hurt God's testimony! Paul reminded the church at Rome of the same unfortunate circumstance: "For the name of God is blasphemed among the Gentiles through you" (Romans 2:24).

Years ago, Dr. Bill Rice was holding a revival meeting in a smaller community. He had his wife and small children with him, and the church was housing him in a home a couple of blocks from the church. One night after the preaching, Dr. Rice was talking with some of the people and counseling them as an evangelist might typically do. The children, however, were tired, so Mrs. Rice informed her husband that she was going to leave so that she could put the children to bed. Dr. Rice told her that he would be done soon and join her at the house in a few minutes.

After finishing up at the church, Dr. Rice walked the two blocks or so to the house and upon arrival found that the children were already asleep and his wife was readying herself for bed as well. She said, "Bill, we could use a couple of items for breakfast if you wouldn't mind getting them." He said, "No problem; what do you need?" His wife told him, "A loaf of bread and some milk."

Dr. Rice grabbed his wallet and headed down the street in the opposite direction from the church to a little corner market that he assumed might still be open. Upon arriving, he was delighted to find a lady tending the store. He stepped inside and proceeded to pick out a loaf of bread and a gallon of milk. He set them on the counter and took out his wallet.

The lady reached under the counter and pulled out a *Playboy* magazine, set it on the counter in front of the evangelist, and said, "Would you like anything else, Sir?"

Dr. Rice was startled by this sudden temptation and immediately bounced his eyes off of the magazine on the counter and looked squarely at the lady and said, "No, ma'am." She responded by pushing the magazine a little closer to him and saying, "Are you sure?" "I'm absolutely sure," said the evangelist, "Just the bread and the milk, please. What's the total?"

The cashier placed the magazine under the counter and quickly added up the total of the two items and placed them into a paper bag. Dr. Rice handed her some money, received his change, and headed for the door with his bag of groceries. As he reached for the handle on the door, the lady said, "Have a good evening, Evangelist Rice!" She had been in the service that night and had heard him preach. She decided to put him to a test. He passed!

As a college instructor, I love to inform students that they did well on a test or exam. I enjoy seeing their expressions of joy over success. But when a student fails, I'm reluctant to tell them. I wonder if the same is true in life. People all around us put our testimonies to the test. When we pass, they most likely will inform us; but if we fail they no doubt keep it to themselves and chalk it up as another hypocrite who says one thing and lives something else. We must protect the ground of our individual testimonies!

DEFEND THE TRUTH

We are part of a cause bigger than ourselves. Jude 3 says, "Beloved, when I gave all diligence to write unto you of the common salvation, it was needful for me to write unto you, and exhort you that ye should earnestly contend for the faith which was once delivered unto the saints." "The faith" here refers to a set of beliefs—our doctrine. Each of us as individuals is responsible to protect the doctrine that defines our faith.

The Apostle Paul took this challenge seriously.

...a dispensation of the gospel is committed unto me.
—1 CORINTHIANS 9:17

Whereof I am made a minister, according to the dispensation of God which is given to me for you, to fulfill the word of God.—COLOSSIANS 1:25

But as we were allowed of God to be put in trust with the gospel, even so we speak; not as pleasing men, but God, which trieth our hearts.—1 THESSALONIANS 2:4

According to the glorious gospel of the blessed God, which was committed to my trust.—1 TIMOTHY 1:11

Will we be the generation that allows truth to fall in the street? Will we be the generation that fails to get the gospel to every creature? Under our watch will local churches close their doors? Will we live and die without a revival?

We stand in a long line of battle tested saints—the Old Testament prophets, Jesus' disciples, the early church martyrs, the Reformers, the Pilgrims, the evangelists of the two Great Awakenings, the pioneer church planters, and the modern day pastors and missionaries who have refused to compromise truth no matter what the personal cost. We simply must not give up the ground that they so valiantly have claimed.

We have ground to protect—but how is it possible? The battle seems more intense than ever, and, as we have seen, we are no match against the enemy in this spiritual warfare. How can we protect anything?

THE ARMOR OF GOD

Twice in Ephesians 6, God exhorts us to access the "whole armour of God" (vv. 11, 13). There are six pieces of armor listed, and we must have all of them at all times. As we finish this chapter, we will look at five of these necessary elements in the armor. (We'll devote an entire chapter to the sixth element because it comes with a special admonition.)

As we look at each component, remember, we must "put on" this armor—all of it—every day!

Put on a Reliable Word

The first area of armor that God insists we put on is a reliable word: "Stand therefore, having your loins girt about with truth" (Ephesians 6:14).

When we lie, we play right into the hands of the "father of lies." God insists on honesty among His people: "These are the things that ye shall do; Speak ye every man the truth to his neighbour; execute the judgment of truth and peace in your gates" (Zechariah 8:16). "Wherefore putting away lying, speak every man truth with his neighbour: for we are members one of another" (Ephesians 4:25).

It is said that the average person lies between six and ten times a day. Are you honest?

Are you honest with yourself? We often tell the biggest lies to ourselves. We know that we have sin in our lives, but we excuse it or justify it in some way. We lie to ourselves about our sin and its consequences.

Are you honest with God? Someone has rightly said that more lying takes place during the song service in church than anywhere else! We often sing the words of songs but don't mean them. We pray prayers that we don't mean. We kneel at an altar perhaps in order to look good, but fail to keep our vows. Again, God is very explicit here: "When thou vowest a vow unto God, defer not to pay it; for he hath no pleasure in fools: pay that which thou hast vowed. Better is it that thou shouldest not vow, than thou shouldest vow and not pay. Suffer not thy mouth to cause thy flesh to sin; neither say thou before the angel, that it was an error: wherefore should God be angry at thy voice, and destroy the work of thine hands?" (Ecclesiastes 5:4–6).

Are we honest with those around us? Do we keep our promises to our family and friends? Do we embellish our testimonies to make ourselves look better than someone else? It's tempting to pad our résumé in some way to get ahead at work or be dishonest in our business dealings. The writer of Hebrews asked others to pray that his life and ministry would represent the truth: "Pray for us: for we trust we have a good conscience, in all things willing to live honestly" (Hebrews 13:18).

Truthfulness is no small matter. Most of us would place sins related to immorality or murder at the top of God's "abomination list." While it's true that these sins are an abomination to God, we must remember that anything short of the truth is also an abomination to Him: "These six things doth the LORD hate: yea, seven are an abomination unto him:…a lying tongue" (Proverbs 6:16–17). "Lying lips are an abomination to the LORD: but they that deal truly are his delight" (Proverbs 12:22).

To be unfair or deceitful in our dealings with God or man puts us in line for God's judgment, while being honest and just bring His blessings. Proverbs 11:1 says, "A false balance is abomination to the LORD: but a just weight is his delight."

God will not protect a liar! We must gird our loins with truth. Put on a reliable word.

Put on a Righteous Walk

In Ephesians 6:14, God tells us to have "on the breastplate of righteousness." The prophet Isaiah mentions this piece of armor in Isaiah 11:5: "And righteousness shall be the girdle of his loins...." We need a revival of righteousness! "Sow to yourselves in righteousness, reap in mercy; break up your fallow ground: for it is time to seek the LORD, till he come and rain righteousness upon you" (Hosea 10:12). The Apostle Paul called for the church at Corinth to "Awake to righteousness, and sin not; for some have not the knowledge of God: I speak this to your shame" (1 Corinthians 15:34).

We often excuse ourselves from doing right because no one else is, but that is exactly the reason God demands it. God is not surprised when lost people act lost, but He is grieved when saved people do.

We cannot afford to do right once in a while or on Sunday when at the Lord's house. We must develop a pattern of righteousness—doing right at all times, in all situations, to all people. Spiritual maturity is, as Philippians 1:11 says, "Being filled with the fruits of righteousness, which are by Jesus Christ, unto the glory and praise of God."

The standard of righteousness is not the world around us. The above verse links the requirement of doing right to the righteousness of Jesus Christ! Compared to our neighbors, coworkers, or the average Joe on the street, we may be doing fairly well, but how does our way of living compare to the integrity and character of the Lord Jesus Christ?

We may not be able to influence the way our neighbors live, or the way our leaders behave, but we can do something about ourselves. Personal righteousness leads to powerful revival. Proverbs 14:34 observes, "Righteousness exalteth a nation: but sin is a reproach to any people."

Revival starts with me. It is God's finger pointing at me. Gypsy Smith used to say: "If you want revival; go outside and draw a big circle on the ground. Step inside the circle and pray, Lord revive everything in this circle!"

We need our loins protected by truth, and we need to have on the breastplate of righteousness if we plan to win this war.

Put on a Ready Work

The next piece of the armor is found in Ephesians 6:15: "And your feet shod with the preparation of the gospel of peace."

When the legendary basketball coach, John Wooden, of UCLA was conducting basketball camps, he would take an hour at the beginning of the week and teach the young men how to put on their socks. That may sound ridiculous, but Wooden was convinced that your feet provided the foundation for your game and if something wasn't right in the foundation, you would never succeed. One crease or fold in the sock could cause a blister in the first hour of drills that would sideline the player for the rest of camp!

How's your foundation? In studying the life of Christ, we soon discover that the baseline of His coming to this Earth was to bring eternal and abundant life.

I am come that thy might have life, and that they might have it more abundantly.—JOHN 10:10

For the Son of man is come to seek and to save that which was lost.—LUKE 19:10

The Lord's messages throughout the Gospels left us with many duties and responsibilities, but out of them all, one is rightly labeled the Great Commission: "Go ye therefore, and teach all nations, baptizing them in the name of the Father, and of the Son, and of the Holy Ghost: Teaching them to observe all things whatsoever I have commanded you…" (Matthew 28:19–20).

What on your "to-do list" has anything to do with the Great Commission? We call lots of things "ministry" today, but if it doesn't involve leading people to Christ as Saviour, baptizing them, and then discipling them in the Word of God, it is not eternal ministry. We can only take one thing with us from this world when we leave. We won't take our money, or our fame, our church buildings, or the blogs or books that we write. We can only take people. The perpetuation of Christianity depends on our telling others what God has taught us. "And the things that thou hast heard of me among many witnesses, the same commit thou to faithful men, who shall be able to teach others also" (2 Timothy 2:2).

Many today are giving up on soulwinning and discipleship because they think that no one wants our message anymore. The days are too wicked and people are too hard, they say. But that is exactly why we must have our feet shod with the preparation of the gospel of peace. It is *because* "the days are evil" that we must be "redeeming the time" (Ephesians 5:16). Our generation doesn't get a pass on sharing the gospel because of the condition of the lost. People have always been lost! They have always been hard.

The problem is not with the harvest. The problem is a lack of laborers! Jesus in His day saw people without direction and giving up hope, but His response ought to challenge us: "But when he saw the multitudes, he was moved with compassion on them, because they fainted, and were scattered abroad, as sheep having no shepherd. Then saith he unto his disciples, The harvest truly is plenteous, but he labourers are few; Pray ye therefore the Lord of the harvest, that he will send forth labourers into his harvest" (Matthew 9:36–38).

Growing up on the farm, my favorite time of the year was harvest. Whether it was threshing grain, baling hay, or picking corn, I relished the opportunity to work in those fields. Oh, it wasn't easy. I was driving tractors during harvest when I was six years old. I had to stand up and use both feet to push in the clutch to stop the tractor, but I loved it. Baling hay was my favorite. Smelling that freshly mowed alfalfa, throwing those eighty-pound hay bales on a wagon and then unloading them and stacking them in the mow of the barn—there was nothing like it. Our goal was to bring in a thousand bales a day—in between the daily six hours of milking cows plus the daily barn cleaning chores. Those were long days of aching muscles, sunburned skin, and blistered hands, but what a joy at the end of the day to see the fruit of our labor.

My friend, it's harvest season and we must be about our Father's business. Like Christ, we should ever sense the urgency to serve while we have the opportunity: "I must work the works of him that sent me, while it is day: the night cometh, when no man can work" (John 9:4).

If the gospel has come to us, we have an obligation to get it to others. How can we not? "For we cannot but speak the things which we have seen and heard" (Acts 4:20). The Apostle Paul knew that it was not an *option,* but an *obligation* to preach the gospel: "For though I preach the gospel, I have nothing to glory of: for necessity is laid upon me; yea, woe is unto me, if I preach not the gospel!" (1 Corinthians 9:16).

Most people would not consider their feet the most beautiful part of their body. (I know I keep mine covered most of the time.) Interestingly, God considers the feet of the soulwinner beautiful: "…How beautiful are the feet of them that preach the gospel of peace, and bring glad tidings of good things!" (Romans 10:15). Have you put on a "ready work"? A moving target is a lot harder for the devil to hit.

Put on a Recognized Wealth
In Ephesians 6:17, God tells us to put on "the helmet of salvation." Don't let a single day of the battle go by without remembering

where you would be without salvation. "But by the grace of God I am what I am…" (1 Corinthians 15:10).

The longer you are saved the easier it becomes to be deceived about who you are and what you are worth. Jeremiah brings us back to reality in Lamentations 3:22–23: "It is of the LORD's mercies that we are not consumed, because his compassions fail not. They are new every morning: great is thy faithfulness." I find the verse that precedes these two most interesting: "This I recall to my mind, therefore I have hope" (v. 21). You will lose hope in this battle with Satan if you do not recall to your mind the mercies of God that saved you.

A few years back, I jumped in my car after preaching all day in Northern California. I had a four hundred plus mile drive ahead of me, so before getting on the freeway, I decided to fill up with gas and get something to eat in the car. As I approached the interstate there was only one gas station, and it was a no-name brand with a rather dingy looking convenience store. The area wasn't well lit, and, not really knowing if I was in a safe area, I hesitated to pull in. But sensing the urge for junk food, I turned into the lot and up to a pump. As I did, I saw a poorly dressed man on a bicycle pull up alongside of my car. As I got out of the car he said, "Are you rich?" I guess my shirt and tie that I still had on from the services seemed a sure giveaway.

My first thought was that I didn't have time for, nor did I want to be bothered by, some homeless guy on a bike. But as I hesitated in my answer, some words came out of my mouth that, quite frankly, I didn't expect, "Actually, I'm not rich—but my

Father is!" His eyes got huge, and he waited for me as I circled the car to activate the pump and begin filling my car with fuel.

"Really?" he asked.

"Oh yes, He's extremely wealthy."

Not understanding that I meant my Heavenly Father, the man's next question was obvious: "Do you think you could help me out with something to eat? I haven't eaten all day."

I told him, "Let me finish pumping my gas and I'll see what I can do." I went over to the driver's side of my car and reached into the door pocket where I keep some gospel tracts. I grabbed one and handed it to him and told him to sit down on the curb and read it while I finished pumping my gas. He took the pamphlet eagerly and immediately sat down on the island that housed the gas pumps. He never looked up as I finished pumping the gas and went in to the convenience store. Inside, I purchased two hotdogs, two bags of chips, and two bottles of soda. When I came back to my car he was still reading. I sat down next to him and said, "I got you a couple of things—I hope it helps." With tears in his eyes, he held the tract toward me and said, "Thank you for this." I asked if he had read it already and he responded with an excited "Yes! I prayed this prayer at the end as well." Then he added, "I'm going to Heaven!"

He took the food I had purchased for him but he didn't seem hungry anymore. He followed me to the door of my car and said "thank you" three or four times before I pulled away. I didn't need my hot dog or chips to keep me awake that night! I was thankful God had crossed my path with this man.

You may not have much in this life but if you remember that you have eternal life—you'll stay encouraged in the battle. "For we know that if our earthly house of this tabernacle were dissolved, we have a building of God, an house not made with hands, eternal in the heavens" (2 Corinthians 5:1). We will one day go "To an inheritance incorruptible, and undefiled, and that fadeth not away, reserved in heaven for you" (1 Peter 1:4).

It was this recognized wealth of salvation that enabled Paul to say, "For to me to live is Christ, and to die is gain" (Philippians 1:21).

Put on the Right Weapon

Ephesians 6:17 tells us another piece of armor to put on: "…and the sword of the Spirit, which is the word of God." Remember what I wrote earlier: we can't out-smart, out-muscle, out-run, or out-shout Satan, but we can out-truth him! There is no truth in Satan according to John 8:44. If you know one Bible verse you have more truth than your enemy.

I am so thankful that God has entrusted us with truth and has preserved it for us in His Word: "Thy word is truth" (John 17:17). "Thy word is true from the beginning: and every one of thy righteous judgments endureth for ever" (Psalm 119:160).

Is your weapon ready? Satan will not give you time to call your pastor as he lines up another fiery dart. You won't have time to check your concordance or even get out your Bible. You must have the weapon of truth in your heart.

Wherewithal shall a young man cleanse his way? by taking heed thereto according to thy word. With my whole heart have I sought thee: O let me not wander from thy commandments. Thy word have I hid in mine heart, that I might not sin against thee.—PSALM 119:9–11

The word is night thee, even in thy mouth, and in thy heart.—ROMANS 10:8

The sword of the Spirit is a powerful and proven weapon against the onslaught of Satan. "For the word of God is quick, and powerful, and sharper than any twoedged sword, piercing even to the dividing asunder of soul and spirit, and of the joints and marrow, and is a discerner of the thoughts and intents of the heart" (Hebrews 4:12). If we will use this powerful weapon, God will do the rest: "The prophet that hath a dream, let him tell a dream; and he that hath my word, let him speak my word faithfully. What is the chaff to the wheat? saith the LORD? Is not my word like as a fire? saith the LORD; and like a hammer that breaketh the rock in pieces?" (Jeremiah 23:28–29).

So let's review. Do you have the provision of grace? Have you established your relationship with Jesus Christ? Remember, relationships require two people. Would God call you a Christian? "The Spirit itself beareth witness with our spirit, that we are the children of God" (Romans 8:16). If you have been born again, are you relying on your power or the power of God?

Are you protecting ground? We each have an individual testimony to protect but also collectively we have an inherited treasure that we must guard carefully. Satan has been given way too much ground in recent days. We must stand. We must fight. We must hold our ground.

Are you equipped with the armor of God? Did you fail to put it—even a piece of it—on today? You can be sure that Satan will be shooting at that unprotected place. Are you telling the truth? Are you living righteously? Are you sharing the gospel? Are you remembering your salvation? Do you have your weapon ready?

TAKE NO CHANCES

Ron Brooks was a Major in the United States Army and became a decorated helicopter pilot during the Korean War. After the war, he finished his education and took a position as an assistant pastor in South Carolina.

During the Vietnam War, Major Brooks received a call from the Army and was informed that he must report for duty. It was not easy to leave his family and ministry, but Uncle Sam gave him no choice.

For two terms in the Vietnam War, Ron served as the lead helicopter pilot for the Army. His job was to fly into an area ahead of our troops and lay down a heavy fog so other choppers could deliver soldiers to war-torn areas. Obviously, these missions were dangerous. He was shot down on more than one occasion and only by God's grace lived to tell the stories.

Ron's co-pilot was a man by the name of Sandy. He was an excellent pilot, but he was unsaved…and knew it. Ron had shared the gospel with Sandy on many occasions and prayed earnestly that he would come to Christ.

One particular morning, the pair received orders to fly into a dangerous area and lay the fog cover for the troops to follow. Their normal procedure was to take the chopper up for a trial run early in the morning and then return to base for a light breakfast before flying the mission. After the early morning ritual and landing the helicopter, Ron looked at Sandy and said, "This is going to be dangerous Sandy. We may not make it through this one. Have you thought any more about getting saved? You won't have a better opportunity than right now to trust Christ."

Sandy looked at Ron and said, "Look, what you are telling me makes sense. I know that I'm a sinner and I need Christ to save me, but my mind is on this mission. When we get back, let's talk about it." Ron pressed him further about the urgency of the matter and begged him not to put it off, but Sandy opened the door of the chopper and headed for breakfast.

The mission that day did not go well. They were hit almost immediately upon entering the war zone, and the chopper was faltering badly. Pummeled by enemy artillery, Ron and Sandy, two of the best of the best, managed to fly that handicapped aircraft to safety. After an awkward landing, an exhausted pilot looked over at his co-pilot and said, "Sandy, we made it!" There was no response or movement. A trickle of bright red blood was running down the side of Sandy's neck. Ron reached over and pulled up his co-pilot's helmet, only to find that Sandy had been fatally wounded. A bullet to the neck just beneath the helmet had taken his life. One small unprotected area was all it took for the enemy to claim a casualty of war.

When the Army did an investigation of the helicopter, it was found that the bullet that killed Sandy that day had entered the chopper in a direct flight toward Ron, the pilot. Upon entering the aircraft, however, the bullet hit a tiny screw on the side of the steering mechanism and was deflected in the direction of the co-pilot instead. God had miraculously spared the life of His servant, but Sandy, without the grace of God and the protection of God was left vulnerable.

Don't take that same chance in spiritual warfare. God has provided spiritual armor for us, but we must diligently put each piece of it on every day.

CHAPTER FIVE

The Confidence that Wins

The moment we get saved we enter spiritual warfare. This is a battle we cannot win on our own with our human defense mechanisms. And yet, God has given us His protection—armor for the battle. As we saw in our previous chapter, we must put it on every day.

Once armed, we must "above all" take the shield of faith (Ephesians 6:16). I have saved this final piece of God's provision for a separate chapter because of those two words "above all." This phrase does not indicate that the shield is more important than the rest of the armor but that it is in addition to the rest. Or, "in all things" we must have this shield of protection. At no time in the battle can we afford to drop our shield.

The shield referred to here was not a tiny little piece of metal that would protect only the head or vital organs in the chest area. This was an oblong, full-body shield that a heavily armed soldier would carry. Behind it was a man fully protected. This shield was wooden so the fiery darts would sink in far enough for the bulb of burning liquid to be broken and thus the fire extinguished and the poison spilled with no effect.

What is this shield that the child of God needs "above all" or "in all things" or "in every area"? It is the shield of faith! Many a Christian has lost the battle because he forgot his shield.

When Jesus was here on Earth, He pondered: "...when the Son of man cometh, shall he find faith on the earth?" (Luke 18:8). Perhaps Jesus saw the shields dropping in His time and wondered if anyone would be walking by faith when He would return for His children.

Our day makes it easy to "walk by sight" rather than walking by faith. Technology allows us to preview before we print. That works great when printing a letter, but that isn't the way God commanded us to live. Hebrews 10:38 says, "Now the just shall live by faith...." In the following chapter, God defines faith for us: "Now faith is the substance of things hoped for, the evidence of things not seen" (Hebrews 11:1). Christians sometimes tell me, "I just don't see how I can live a victorious life" or "I don't see how we can have revival in these days" or "I don't see how I can afford to tithe." According to God's Word, we're not supposed to be able to "see" it! If we can see it, it's not faith!

In John 6:28, the disciples asked Jesus, "What shall we do, that we might work the works of God?" Now that's a great question and one that we might ask. We may phrase it any number of ways, depending on the specific "works of God" we want to see: *What can we do to get our church to grow? What can I do to kick this stubborn habit? What can we do to have revival? What can we do to plant more churches or get more missionaries to the foreign field?*

The disciples asked a good question indeed. *And* they were asking the right Person! If anyone could give them an answer about what they could do, it would be Jesus Christ.

Christ's answer to this intriguing question is astounding: "Jesus answered and said unto them, This is the work of God, that ye believe on him whom he hath sent" (John 6:29). *This* is your work, Jesus said, "...that ye believe!"

How can I kick this stubborn habit? What can we do to have revival? What can we do to plant more churches or get more missionaries to the foreign field? Jesus said, "...that ye believe!" Your work is faith!

Are you walking by faith? Are you living by faith? Are you praying in faith? Are you giving by faith? Are you serving by faith? To serve without faith is to serve sinfully. To live the Christian life without faith is to live in sin. To give by what we can see to give is to sin as we give. No wonder the writer of Hebrews said, "But without faith it is impossible to please him: for he that cometh to God must believe that he is, and that he is a rewarder of them that diligently seek him" (Hebrews 11:6).

Have you dropped the shield of faith? There are several reasons why soldiers in spiritual warfare drop the shield of faith, but there is one very good reason we must hold it high—to win!

ABOVE ALL DOUBT

I have the privilege of teaching on the college level. It is my passion to get students to think, and I rejoice over the great minds that I'm privileged to challenge on a daily basis. But I often warn my students that it is easy to lose God in intellectualism and scholasticism. We cannot understand everything about God academically. In Isaiah 55:8–9 God declares, "For my thoughts are not your thoughts, neither are your ways my ways saith the LORD. For as the heavens are higher than the earth, so are my ways higher than your ways, and my thoughts than your thoughts."

Many brilliant minds have studied the Bible and come away skeptics and critics. There is something missing in their search for knowledge. It is as Isaiah 47:10 says: "…Thy wisdom and thy knowledge, it hath perverted thee; and thou hast said in thine heart, I am, and none else beside me."

Wisdom and knowledge can thwart your quest for God because our finite brains cannot comprehend the infinite wisdom and knowledge of God. We are informed by God Himself that He has not chosen to reveal everything to us. "The secret things belong unto the LORD our God…" (Deuteronomy 29:29). So what do we do when we don't understand God? We pick up the shield of faith!

My mind cannot comprehend the eternality of God. How does something exist today without a beginning? How can someone have always existed and never cease to exist? These are questions beyond my human understanding. Though I've tried, I still find it difficult to fully explain the Trinity. Have you ever tried to explain the virgin birth to a child? Critics love to poke at these areas and attempt to destroy our beliefs. But this is where we pick up the shield of faith.

In Hebrews 6, God briefly reviews the covenant that He made with Abraham back in the Book of Genesis. God told him that he would indeed have a son even though he was ninety-nine years old and his wife ninety! Both Abraham and Sarah had their doubts as they were well past the age of bearing children. God knew they were struggling with His promise and He would have gladly given them evidence that He would keep His word. But there was no witness greater than God Himself: "For when God made promise to Abraham, because he could swear by no greater, he sware by himself" (Hebrews 6:13). In effect, God said, "Abraham, I'd like to give you some other proof that I'm going to do what I promised, but since there is no one greater than Me—just take My word for it—by faith!"

Thank God we can take His word for it! God said it—that settles it, whether or not I can academically understand it. "God is not a man, that he should lie; neither the son of man, that he should repent: hath he said, and shall he not do it? or hath he spoken, and shall he not make it good?" (Numbers 23:19).

FIGHTS TO AVOID

Sometimes I'm not really sure what to call all of the "Christian" conversation today. In many circles there seems to be an argumentative spirit, while in others there is a one-better-than-you response, while in some others there just seems to be an exorbitant amount of time wasted over non-essentials. I believe God labels all of it—carnal. "For ye are yet carnal: for whereas there is among you envying, and strife, and divisions, are ye not carnal, and walk as men?" (1 Corinthians 3:3).

Now I enjoy a good discussion about Scripture or a theological or biblical issue with my co-laborers in the ministry. But the email debates and self-promoting blogs are causing self-destruction over matters that don't matter.

God clearly tells us to avoid these quarrels: "But foolish and unlearned questions avoid, knowing that they do gender strifes" (2 Timothy 2:23). "Neither give heed to fables and endless genealogies, which minister questions, rather than godly edifying which is **in faith**: so do" (1 Timothy 1:4). Did you notice the words "in faith"? If you want to fight—fight the good fight of faith!

I'm not against studying and stretching our minds in theological matters, but when there is a carnal spirit involved in the discussion, I'd rather use my energy to fight Satan than fight some seminary. The more faith that I have in God and His Word, the less I'm concerned about debates that have been waged for centuries and are still unsolved. The battle is being lost while carnal Christians quarrel.

QUESTIONS AND QUAGMIRES

Why do good Christian people suffer with cancer? Why do wars take the lives of innocent people? Why doesn't God prevent natural disaster? Why did that baby die? Why can't that fine single lady find a life partner? Have you found yourself asking these and similar questions? We are often at a loss, but if we hang around in faith for a while, God will show us.

I love the insight of Daniel as he speaks about God. "He revealeth the deep and secret things: he knoweth what is in the darkness, and the light dwelleth with him" (Daniel 2:22). Paul certainly had his trials and curve balls thrown his way in life and ministry, but in Romans 8:28 he records for us a wonderful promise: "And we know that all things work together for good to them that love God, to them who are the called according to his purpose."

We see life from the playing field, but God sees it from the blimp. When I played football in high school and college, I often couldn't comprehend in the middle of a game why the coach would give a particular instruction. It just didn't seem like what he was asking was possible or that it would help us win the game. But on Monday night in those film sessions I could see it plainly. What seemed impossible and difficult on the playing field looked completely different from a higher perspective. By faith we can always trust God in the quagmires of life.

Sometimes we drop our shield of faith because of the questions and doubts in our heads. But sometimes, perhaps more often, we do it because of a problem in our hearts.

A DIVIDED HEART

A divided heart will always lead to a defeated life. You can't have your cake and eat it too. "No man can serve two masters: for either he will hate the one, and love the other; or else he will hold to the one, and despise the other…" (Matthew 6:24). "Ye cannot drink the cup of the Lord, and the cup of devils: ye cannot be partakers of the Lord's table, and of the table of devils" (1 Corinthians 10:21). This is why James 4:8 instructs, "Cleanse your hands ye sinners; and purify your hearts, ye double minded."

How do we keep from riding the fence? How do we prevent duplicity when it comes to our loyalty? With the shield of faith! Faith will shield us from the selfishness of our own hearts.

Selfishness always aborts surrender. My will must be in full surrender to His way. Our biggest enemy is our selves! D.L. Moody used to say, "The man I fear the most is the one who walks underneath this hat."

When God predicted the peril of the end times and pointed to the conditions of the last days, He did not mention crime, political corruption, war, or violence. His words stick a dagger into the heart of every one of us! "For men shall be lovers of their own selves…" (2 Timothy 3:2).

Romans 1:25 describes our day, but, sadly, it also describes what is often the condition of our own hearts as well: "Who changed the truth of God into a lie, and worshipped and served the creature more than the Creator, who is blessed for ever. Amen." Paul sadly states in Philippians 2:21, "For all seek their own, not the things which are Jesus Christ's."

We badly need some funerals for self. "I die daily" (1 Corinthians 15:31) was the cry of the Apostle Paul. Elsewhere he declared, "I am crucified with Christ: nevertheless I live; yet not I, but Christ liveth in me: and the life which I now live in the flesh I live by the faith of the Son of God, who loved me, and gave himself for me" (Galatians 2:20).

To hold the shield of faith, we must surrender our selfish desires.

FLESHLY TEMPTATIONS

Sensual folly causes shields to fall! God could have made us like the angels who are non-sexual, but He designed us at creation as sexual beings. The sexual temptations in our culture continually press upon us. To live in victory over fleshly fulfillments, we must believe and claim the promise in 1 Corinthians 10:13: "There hath no temptation taken you but such as is common to man: but God is faithful, who will not suffer you to be tempted above that ye are able; but will with the temptation also make a way to escape, that ye may be able to bear it."

It takes faith to walk in the Spirit, but when we do we will not fulfill the lusts of the flesh. (See Galatians 5:16.) The disease of sensual addiction must be put to death. "And they that are Christ's have crucified the flesh with the affections and lusts" (Galatians 5:24). We cannot afford to take a casual approach to this onslaught of temptation. We must "Flee also youthful lusts: but follow…faith" (2 Timothy 2:22).

I know this age is filled with temptation and it is easy to think that God doesn't expect us to take the same moral stance that they did back in the New Testament, or in other times past. But think about the words in Titus 2:12: "Teaching us that, denying ungodliness and worldly lusts, we should live soberly, righteously, and godly, in this present world." The command to live godly and separate from fleshly sins is timeless, and we must heed it today.

SPIRITUAL DISSATISFACTION

The moment you are convinced that God is somehow not being good to you, you will drop your shield of faith. Why would you trust someone who has, in your mind, let you down? Often people reject Christ as their Saviour because they believe God has wronged them or been unfair to them in some way.

Years ago I was preaching a revival in Cody, Wyoming. On Sunday night a lady approached me after the service and told me how she had gotten saved just a few months previous. She was deeply burdened for her husband, however, who was lost and claimed to be an atheist. She asked if I would come and talk to him. I asked about a good time to catch him, and she informed me that he walked home from work every noon hour for lunch and was always home from noon until 1:00 PM.

The next day, the pastor and I just happened to knock on his door around 12:15 PM. Herb invited us in as long as we were okay with him eating lunch in our presence. As we talked about his wife attending the church, etc., and giving him an invitation to the revival, I asked Herb whether he was 100 percent sure he would go to Heaven if he were to die. He responded with, "I'm an atheist." I said, "Well, Herb, that is interesting. You know,

I'm a Christian, but I haven't always been a Christian. One day I became a Christian and if you were to ask me how that happened I would love to tell you. But I'm interested in you. Surely you haven't always been an atheist. Would you mind telling me when you became an atheist?"

He sat up straight and put his sandwich down. He said, "When I was a boy my parents abandoned me and I ended up living with and being raised by my grandmother. I loved her very much as she was the only family I had. When I was in seventh grade, I came home from school one afternoon and found the police at my house. They said that my grandmother had been taken to the hospital and was very sick. They put me in the patrol car and took me to her room. She was hooked up to all kinds of machines and couldn't talk. I sat there and I prayed that if there was a God, He would not let my grandmother die." He paused, and with tears now in his eyes, he said, "Mr. Goetsch, she died that night and I decided at that moment that there was no God because He didn't hear my prayer."

I opened my Bible and began to explain how when Jesus was on the Earth He would often come in contact with people who were blind, or lame, or had lost a loved one. Through these difficult circumstances time and again Jesus would show His love to them. It was through these hardships that they recognized their need for a Saviour. As Herb listened intently, I shared the plan of salvation. When I got to the part about Christ dying for us, he looked at me and said, "You know, I don't think I'm an atheist—I think I need Jesus as my Saviour." What a joy it was to see Herb trust Christ that day in his kitchen.

Has your heart become divided because you don't understand some event in your life? Pick up the shield of faith!

> *Trust in the LORD with all thine heart; and lean not unto thine own understanding. In all thy ways acknowledge him, and he shall direct thy paths.*—PROVERBS 3:5–6

> *Thou wilt keep him in perfect peace, whose mind is stayed on thee: because he trusteth in thee. Trust ye in the LORD forever: for in the LORD JEHOVAH is everlasting strength.*—ISAIAH 26:3–4

KEEP MOVING

The spiritual warfare in which we find ourselves is for a lifetime. This is not a short skirmish; there is no demilitarized zone; no cease fires; no truces. It is war day in and day out until the trumpet sounds for the Rapture or God calls us home. No one gets through this battle unscathed. There will be some injuries. At some time or another you will be hit by a fiery dart. With God's help, we can recover, but those battle wounds can have long range effects.

I was fortunate to get through ten years of football without any serious injuries. But those bumps and bruises? I feel them now. When my right shoulder aches or my left elbow throbs or my right Achilles heel tightens up, I can tell you the game and the yard line on the field where the injury occurred. Over the years, arthritis has set in.

Spiritual warfare is like that. The devil is patient—willing over time to keep attacking. That's why God admonishes us in Galatians 6:9: "And let us not be weary in well doing: for in due season we shall reap, if we faint not."

As I was driving away from the airport parking lot in Los Angeles one evening, I saw in the distance a large green billboard with one word printed in giant white letters. It was the word ARTHRITIS. I thought it to be a rather odd title for a movie, so I kept my eye on it as I got closer. There were small letters beneath that giant word that simply said: "Keep moving." There is no cure for arthritis, and doctors will tell you that, as painful as it may be, the best thing to do is "keep moving." Hebrews 12:1 exhorts us to run our race with "patience" or endurance. This is a marathon battle—keep moving to the finish line.

AVOID SPIRITUAL ATROPHY

Physical atrophy often takes place when a part of our body is placed into a cast because of a fractured bone. Due to a lack of use and activity, the muscles atrophy. When the cast is taken off, it takes some time for those muscles to be rehabilitated to full use once again. But atrophy can also take place when an insufficient amount of blood, water, oxygen, or nutrients are getting to a muscle or nerve area.

Bo Jackson was one of the greatest athletes to ever play professional sports. He was multi-talented, and after winning the Heisman trophy at Auburn his senior year he entered the

NFL. But he was also drafted by the Kansas City Royals of Major League Baseball. Most athletes at that point would have to make a choice. Not Bo—he chose both football and baseball. He played baseball for the Royals and football for the Oakland Raiders—at the same time. That's right; he would play football with the Raiders on Sunday and then fly to wherever the Royals were playing and play baseball during the week.

ESPN recently did a documentary on the injury that brought a sudden end to Bo Jackson's career. He was running down the sideline of the football field and was tackled from behind by a player who had taken a proper angle of pursuit. Because Bo was running so fast and hard, when the tackler caught his legs and pulled them the other way, his hip was dislocated. Bo went face down to the ground and lay there for a moment in pain. As trainers and fellow players rushed to him, he rolled over on to his back. Later, it was discovered that when he did, his hip went back into its socket.

Teammates helped Bo to his feet, and he limped to the sideline in pain, but the pain was not as severe as at the original contact. After the game, he assumed he had a bruised hip or a hip pointer of some kind. No MRI was done as he actually felt pretty good. But for weeks Bo stayed on the sideline of both his careers because he just could not seem to get any strength back in his hip. For over a year he tried to rehabilitate his hip, but to no avail.

It was finally discovered by an MRI that when Bo rolled over onto his back and his hip went back into position, some blood vessels were pinched, and as a result no blood was able to get to his hip socket. Over time, all life in that socket died, and the career of an amazing athlete was over for good.

You may not think that missing a day of Bible reading will hurt you. After all, what's the big deal about being in church every service? Friend, you are denying yourself the life flow that is necessary for your spiritual health.

If you're not growing, you're slowing. Spiritual atrophy will cause you to drop the shield of faith, and once you do—you're a prime target for the fiery darts of the wicked one. Keep the nutrients of God's Word flowing into your life. "As newborn babes, desire the sincere milk of the word, that ye may grow thereby" (1 Peter 2:2). "Not forsaking the assembling of ourselves together, as the manner of some is; but exhorting one another: and so much the more, as ye see the day approaching" (Hebrews 10:25).

Stop the excuses for missing church, time in God's Word, Christian fellowship, and service! This battle demands soldiers who are strong in the Lord. Damaged hands always drop shields.

THE DANGER OF DEPLETED HOPE

Rufus Jones once said, "There is no future for the man whose faith has burned out." The minute you think this war is lost—you'll drop your shield and become a casualty. Fatalism is depleting our ranks today. William Booth, the founder of the Salvation Army, said: "Look well to the fire of your soul, for it is always the tendency of fire to go out."

We often use the word *hope* in a different way than the Bible does. We would say, "I hope it doesn't rain today." We have no real assurance about what the weather will do; we simply have a preference that it doesn't rain and so we hope that it doesn't. But when the Bible uses the word *hope* it speaks of a "confident expectation." Listen to what Paul said in Titus 2:13: "Looking for that blessed hope, and the glorious appearing of the great God and our Saviour Jesus Christ." Paul was not thinking that the Lord may or may not come back. He knew beyond a shadow of a doubt—it was the blessed hope! We must not allow the fire of this hope to die in our souls.

We Must Have Faith in Life-Changing Regeneration

Do you believe that salvation is the answer? Are you convinced that the gospel changes lives, changes homes, changes communities, and can change a nation? God does! Second Corinthians 5:17 says, "Therefore if any man be in Christ, he is a new creature: old things are passed away; behold, all things are become new."

Al Capone was a notorious gangster in the city of Chicago back in the 1920s and '30s. George Mensick was a bodyguard of Capone as they carried out their criminal activity. Mensick told how the gang would buy a new Cadillac every week and at the end of seven days would burn it in a vacant lot to keep the police from knowing what they were driving. Most of the time high on drugs or drunk with alcohol, George would stagger home to his apartment and beat his wife and little girl.

One night, as he entered the apartment, he was so out of his mind that he took out his gun and hit his wife with the handle knocking her out cold. Thinking that he had killed her he headed to the bedroom of his little four-year old girl intending to shoot her in her sleep. But as he opened the door, he was sobered by the sight of his little girl kneeling by the side of her bed praying. "Dear Jesus, Please save my Daddy! Please save my Daddy!" was her prayer. George Mensick dropped the gun and then dropped to his knees and trusted the Saviour about whom his precious wife had so faithfully told him.

Brother Mensick became an evangelist, and he ate a number of meals in our home when I was a boy. I heard him give his testimony many times. He dedicated his life to reaching people for Christ and especially those who were incarcerated. He had access to every prison in the country and led many on death row to Christ. I had the privilege of meeting him again just a few months before he died. What a wonderful testimony he was to the powerful grace of God. Don't ever lose hope in life changing regeneration!

We Must Have Faith in Spirit-Enabled Righteous Living

I wonder what would happen if God's people would have no other gods in their lives but the one true God. What if we stopped taking God's name in vain? What would our country be like if professing Christians would honor the Lord's day and be in a local church for worship and service? What would happen if children obeyed their parents, if we stopped killing, committing adultery, stealing, lying, and coveting? What if we just did what is right? Proverbs 14:34 answers that question succinctly: "Righteousness exalteth a nation: but sin is a reproach to any people."

You may think, "But I'm just one person." One person makes a difference! When Joshua did right, his family did right. When Jonah did right, a city did right. When Josiah did right, a nation did right. The politicians haven't been successful in changing our nation for the better. The environmentalists, sociologists, philosophers, psychologists, authors, and musicians have all had their chances. Why don't we try God? Let's just give the Ten Commandments a shot. Doing right doesn't start with my neighbor—it starts with me!

We Must Have Faith in Compassionate Religion

I am not referring to modern day religion here, but the religion spoken of in James 1:27: "Pure religion and undefiled before God and the Father is this, To visit the fatherless and widows in their affliction, and to keep himself unspotted from the world." When was the last time we ministered to a widow in the church or a kid without a dad? The implication here is that we are to care for those who are less fortunate than we are and meet their needs. It's not the government's job to take care of these people—it is ours!

How about spiritually? Have we visited a spiritual widow lately—someone without the Bridegroom coming for them in the Rapture? There are certainly many spiritually fatherless children for us to visit—those without a heavenly Father.

Ministry is *people* work rather than *paper* work, and each of us as individuals needs to get back to caring about the needs of others. We can make a difference in people's lives through loving, compassionate religion. Jude 22 says, "And of some have compassion, making a difference." I want to be one of those compassionate difference makers.

We Must Have Faith in Local Church Revival

I was preaching on revival one evening at a camp where I have been privileged to speak since 1977. The director, a good friend who has heard me preach many times, came up afterwards and said, "John, whenever I hear you preach on revival, you sound as though you believe we can actually have one. What do you see today in the world that makes you believe we can have revival?"

I didn't really think about my response as it came somewhat unexpectedly: "I don't see anything. In fact, I see just the opposite. But I don't have to see something to believe that it can happen." "Now faith is the substance of things hoped for, the evidence of things not seen" (Hebrews 11:1).

So many today look at the conditions of our culture and decide that it is too late for God to work. But every major revival in the Bible and in history has come on the heels of financial, moral, and spiritual collapse. The conditions were not ripe for revival in Elijah's day under King Ahab and his wife Jezebel. No one would have predicted revival in Josiah's lifetime as he comes to the throne at the age of eight with fifty-seven years of idolatrous worship preceding him. Nineveh was not hungry for God, nor were the people on the day of Pentecost. Paul ministered under the wicked reign of Nero, yet saw miraculous conversions, churches established, and Christians growing.

God's Word and the promises of revival still stand today: "If my people, which are called by my name, shall humble themselves, and pray, and seek my face, and turn from their wicked ways; then will I hear from heaven, and will forgive their sin, and will heal their land" (2 Chronicles 7:14). "And ye shall seek me, and find me, when ye shall search for me with all your heart" (Jeremiah 29:13).

The problem is not with God. The problem is not with the world. The problem is us! And that's good news because we can do something about that! "Sow to yourselves in righteousness, reap in mercy; break up your fallow ground: for it is time to seek the LORD, till he come and rain righteousness upon you" (Hosea 10:12).

PICK UP YOUR SHIELD

"Above all" or "in addition to all" we must take the shield of faith. Remember, "without faith it is impossible to please him: for he that cometh to God must believe that he is, and that he is a rewarder of them that diligently seek him" (Hebrews 11:6).

One night after preaching a message on prayer at a church in Saint Paul, Minnesota, a man approached me in the lobby and asked if he might share a story with me. Of course, I agreed.

This man's mother was saved as a teenager and grew to love the Lord. She met a young man who wasn't a Christian and took an interest in him. She had been taught by this time, however, that she should not marry an unsaved person as that would be an unequal yoke according to Amos 3:3. But the longer she dated him, the more she liked him. The more she liked him, the better she was able to convince herself that she would be able to lead him to Christ after they married.

The man told me that he remembered his mother praying for his dad to be saved every single day as he was growing up. She was faithful to the Lord and to church and led each of her children to Christ, but her husband remained unsaved. "When I was about forty years old," the man continued, "my mother called me one day and said, "Son, you know I have been praying for your dad all these years. I know he is going to get saved. I don't know if it will be in my lifetime, but I am convinced that God will work in his heart and one day he will trust Christ."

He said, "Brother Goetsch, my mother prayed in faith every day for seventy-three years for my dad to be saved. The day after my mother died, my father put his faith in Jesus Christ and was wonderfully saved!"

Faith will keep you in the battle! When you are tempted to doubt or to lose hope, keep believing God and the promises of His Word. "For all the promises of God in him are yea, and in him, Amen, unto the glory of God by us" (2 Corinthians 1:20).

The war is on. It's a lifelong battle; but it can be won! If you've dropped the shield of faith, pick it up once again. "For whatsoever is born of God overcometh the world: and this is the victory that overcometh the world, even our faith" (1 John 5:4).

CONCLUSION

It was a perfect autumn afternoon in Wisconsin. The leaves on the trees were in a splendid array of reds, oranges, and yellows. There was a slight breeze moving the crisp, cool air through Washington Park. It was ideal football weather, and our team was playing Northland College from Ashland, Wisconsin. A few fans were trickling into the park as we positioned ourselves in the west end zone for calisthenics.

Though raised on a dairy farm, my dad was gracious to allow me to play sports. I thoroughly enjoyed football, basketball, and track in high school. When it came time for college, I chose to attend Maranatha Baptist Bible College because they had a football team. At the time, I wasn't right with the Lord and really desired to take a football scholarship at a secular college. God, however, had put me in the hospital my senior year of high school with some heart problems, and I knew that He was speaking to me about serving Him. I wasn't ready to submit, but going to a Bible college in my hometown was my way of a compromise…at least temporarily. I was only intending to go for a year and then take my scholarship.

We had a decent football team in high school, especially my senior year, and I was excited about the prospects of playing at the college level. My freshman year was the first year of football at Maranatha as the school was only two years old. We were only able to schedule four games that first year, and we lost all four. (Although we only lost the last one by a 2–0 score as our quarterback slipped in the end zone and was touched down for a safety near the end of the game against the University of Chicago club team.)

As my sophomore year began, we were thrilled to hear that we had eight games on the schedule, but we were disappointed when only eighteen guys tried out for football. (You need twenty-two players just to practice!) Dr. B. Myron Cedarholm, the president of the college, had been an All-American running back at the University of Minnesota in his college days and had a passion about building a team. He was convinced that football would develop young men in a Bible college setting in a great way for later ministry. I could say much here about my own philosophy about the value of sports to the Christian life, but I'll save that for another time.

That sophomore season was the most difficult time in my life athletically. As I mentioned, we only had eighteen guys on the team. About half of them had not played tackle football in high school. Eight other colleges agreed to play us (everybody needs a "cupcake" on their schedule), and we got hammered every single Saturday. The truth is, we played eight games and never scored once. Not one touchdown all year. No field goals, no safeties, nothing. Zero! We lost by scores of 30–0; 42–0; 55–0; and then there was that Saturday afternoon at Washington Park.

Randy Petersen was a freshman linebacker that year from Colorado. He was an outstanding performer in high school, earning all-state honors. He and I were selected as captains of the team, so we lined up the other sixteen guys in four rows for calisthenics. We were getting loose when all of a sudden I noticed a huge greyhound bus pulling into the parking lot. In bold letters on the side it read "Northland College." I thought, "They have a *bus!* A *greyhound* bus!" We didn't even have a school bus. We didn't even have a home field. (Washington Park was the local high school field that we were renting.) We had to find our own ride to the park—or walk, which is what most of us did.

After accepting the fact that the opponent that day had a nice bus, my anxiety reached new levels when I noticed right behind that bus was a second bus; and behind it were three vans all with "Northland College" boldly written on the side. I thought, "They brought the whole town with them to watch them play!" As the door to the first bus opened, chiseled and muscular young men began unloading. These guys were huge. They had on their game pants and shoes but no shoulder pads or helmets. My jaw dropped when they put on their pads and pulled their jerseys over them. I was seeing numbers like 10, and 22, and 31. These were the skill players—the running backs and defensive backs. When the doors to the second bus opened and the linemen stepped off, I was looking for an exit. I had never seen physical specimens of this nature. And they were mean looking with tattoos, shaved heads, and missing teeth. Ashland, Wisconsin, is in lumber country in the far north of the state, and these guys all looked like they were descendants of Paul Bunyan—or his ox!

Ninety-two football players got off those busses and vans. Ninety two! We had eighteen guys! They lined up in a single file line and walked down one sideline to the other end zone and proceeded to warm up without saying a word. Complete silence. No coaches yelling instructions, no captains calling out drills, nothing—dead silence. I knew we were in trouble. You don't worry about the guy who taunts or talks up a big game before the National anthem—you worry about the guy who just stares! They were staring all right.

Randy and I went out for the toss of the coin, and we won the toss. (It is important for you to remember this because it was the only thing we won all day.) We elected to receive the football which seemed to be the logical thing to do—try to score while we still had eighteen healthy bodies. We all played both ways including special teams, so we lined up in our kick-off receive formation. The ball was kicked near the goal line, but one of our running backs caught it cleanly and started up the sideline. He made it to the fifteen yard line and got absolutely annihilated. He was hit so hard, the ball came loose and Northland recovered.

We turned around to play defense. On the first play from scrimmage, Northland ran a simple dive play off their right guard and easily scored. They kicked the extra point and we went back into kick-off receive mode. This time we managed to hang on to the ball and made it to about the eighteen yard line. On our first offensive snap we threw a little swing pass out into the flat to our flanker, and it was picked off for an interception. The linebacker ran cleanly without being touched into the end zone for another score. Less than thirty seconds into the game, and we were down 14–0. And it got worse!

The score at half time was 62–0. Nine different players had scored touchdowns. They missed one extra point—amazing.

As I was walking off the field, the Northland coach came running over to our sideline and caught up with our head coach. He said, "Coach, this is a mismatch. You're overmatched. This isn't good for you or for us. Our guys over there are getting cocky and your guys, well, they're going to get hurt. Let's just call the game now. It's 62–0—there is no reason to play the second half.

I liked this coach! This was the first logical thing I had heard all day. I wasn't a math major, but I knew 62 plus 62 was 124 and zero and zero is always zero whether you're adding, subtracting, multiplying, or dividing! But our coach said, "No! We will finish this game!" He took us over to the sideline and began to lecture us. "Come on guys," he said, "We can beat this team!" I thought, "Where have you been? Did you go eat a sandwich during the first half? We aren't going to beat anybody today."

We went out for the second half. It didn't get better but Northland did ease up on us some. The final score was 92–0. It was a modern-day record. All of the major newspapers carried the story, and *Sports Illustrated* magazine had an article about the tiny Baptist school that lost a football game ninety-two to nothing! We were the laughing stock of the sports world.

Over four decades later, that game and much of the detail is blurred in my mind, but the hours after are fresh and vivid. I walked into our locker room not wanting to talk to anyone or see anyone. Our locker room was about twenty-five feet by twenty-five feet and had four showers—two of which actually worked. We had two metal folding chairs, and I grabbed one of them and pulled it in front of my locker. With everything but my helmet still on and blood covering my right shin thanks to the 6'4", 280-pound Northland tight end, I sat down and covered my face with my hands.

About an hour passed as the guys showered quietly and left. When I could no longer hear anyone, I slowly pulled my hands from my face only to discover that Randy was sitting on the other folding chair right next to me. He too was still in full pads and had his hands over his face. I put my hand on his shoulder pads and he pulled his hands away from his tear stained face and said, "John, how did that happen? How did we lose a game 92–0?" I just shook my head and mumbled, "I don't know…I don't honestly know."

After a minute or two of just staring at each other in disbelief, I said, "Randy, we can't quit! We can't let these guys quit. They're not going to want to play anymore, but we can't let them quit. This is a great game. We've got to keep going." Randy, who was far more spiritual than I was, began to pray for God's strength and help. That day in that locker room, we vowed that we would stay in the battle.

The next week was tough. Chapel speakers made fun of our football team and told about the story being carried in their local newspapers. Faculty members and students alike laughed at us as we walked the halls. Our roommates were unmerciful. But the season was only half over, so when Monday practice rolled around, Randy and I went through the dorms, study halls, and dating areas, and pulled our football team back on to the practice field.

As stated earlier, we didn't win a game that year—never scored! It was a disaster. I know Dr. Cedarholm was under pressure to cancel the program. Our football team wasn't exactly a good recruiting tool for the college. But the next fall a new season dawned, and we stayed with it. I'll never forget on that same field the next year defeating Martin Luther College from New Ulm, Minnesota, 10–6! *Sports Illustrated* published another article: "School that lost last year 92–0—WINS! It's a miracle!" I had never kicked extra points or field goals prior to that year, but I had the absolute thrill of nailing the extra point and field goal in that game that made the four point difference!

We went on to win again that year and managed a tie in another game. The following year we got three wins and the program was launched. By the way, Northland dropped their football program a few years later due to a lack of interest.

Dr. Cedarholm was right. Those difficult days on the football field prepared us for the spiritual warfare that was ahead in our lives. Randy Petersen is a pastor in Colorado four decades later. One by one those men on that team graduated and went into full-time ministry, and most have remained faithful all these years. Losing had prepared us to win.

You may feel like you're behind in the spiritual battle 92–0. That 6'4", 280-pound fallen angel has been kicking you all over the arena. Don't quit! Victory is coming. The scoreboard says otherwise right now, but that's all about to change.

> *And to you who are troubled rest with us, when the Lord Jesus shall be revealed from heaven with his mighty angels, In flaming fire taking vengeance on them that know not God, and that obey not the gospel of our Lord Jesus Christ: Who shall be punished with everlasting destruction from the presence of the Lord, and from the glory of his power; When he shall come to be glorified in his saints, and to be admired in all them that believe (because our testimony among you was believed) in that day. Wherefore also we pray always for you, that our God would count you worthy of this calling, and fulfill all the good pleasure of his goodness, and the work of faith with power: That the name of our Lord Jesus Christ may be glorified in you, and ye in him, according to the grace of our God and the Lord Jesus Christ.*
> —2 THESSALONIANS 1:7–12

God doesn't just warn us—He is preparing us to win! Stay in the game—I'll see you at the awards ceremony!

Visit us online

strivingtogether.com

wcbc.edu

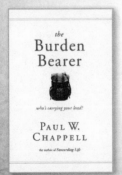

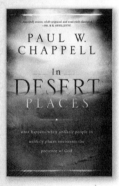